TAROT THERAPY VOLUME 3 – THE MAP OF THE QUEST

By Steve Hounsome

TAROT THERAPY VOLUME 3 – THE MAP OF THE QUEST

© 2012 Steve Hounsome

ISBN 978-1-899878-19-2

CONTENTS

INTRODUCTION..1
CHAPTER 1 – UNFOLDING THE MAP 3
CHAPTER 2 – ORIENTEERING...12
CHAPTER 3 – THE GUIDES ON THE QUEST 22
   PAGES 28
   KNIGHTS..33
   QUEENS 38
   KINGS 44
CHAPTER 4 – THE QUEST 50
   ACES...51
   TWOS..59
   THREES 67
   FOURS 74
   FIVES 81
   SIXES 88
   SEVENS 95
   EIGHTS 102
   NINES..108
   TENS 115
CHAPTER 5 – HOME FROM THE QUEST 122
TAROT THERAPY PRODUCTS..126
BIBLIOGRAPHY 127
BIOGRAPHY 128

INTRODUCTION

This is the third and last Volume of my 'Tarot Therapy' series. The previous two Volumes have explored the theory and practice of Tarot Therapy and the Major Arcana respectively. In this Volume we concern ourselves with the Minor Arcana.

These are often called 'pip' or number cards but as we shall see, that is only half the picture, or one aspect of the card, as if it had been laid flat on the table and is seen only as a one dimensional thing. As readers of the previous two volumes should well know by now, the Tarot is anything but one dimensional, or at least the knowledge or energy it represents is.

Of themselves, Tarot cards are pretty, even profound illustrations of these energies and it is these with which we are concerned in Tarot Therapy. These energies are the underlying, causal reality from which we derive our beings, at all levels. As we saw in Volume 2, the level to which the Major Arcana of the Tarot applies is the whole self, or the transpersonal level – that which goes beyond the boundaries or limits of the different parts of the human being,

So it is with the Minor Arcana we turn our attention to those different aspects or levels. The Major Arcana is the result of the combination of the levels of the human being, a result that is greater than the sum of its parts, in the truly holistic sense, as we have seen. This is in keeping with the quantum nature of reality and reminds us of the majesty of the energy of the Tarot, depicting as it does, the true nature of reality and indeed, our part within this.

The Minor Arcana then shows us the breakdown of the reality, within and without the human being. Seen as energies, as in Tarot Therapy we must, the four suits of the Minor Arcana relate to the levels of the human being in or from which we move, live and have our being. This structure is perhaps most easily seen in grid form, as below:

1

SUIT	ELEMENT	LEVEL
PENTACLES	EARTH	PHYSICAL
CUPS	WATER	EMOTIONAL
SWORDS	AIR	MENTAL
RODS	FIRE	SPIRITUAL

We can see from this that the Minor Arcana is the framework upon which the Major Arcana sits. Put more poetically, the Major Arcana tells us why we undertake the individual quest of our lives whilst the Minor Arcana tells us how. So it is we can see the Minor Arcana as the map that guides us through the misty mountains and deathly hollows we are each bound to encounter as we live our life and hopefully seek to progress and develop ourselves to be the best we can be. How good it is to have such a map with us all the time, a pack of cards we can turn to when our way seems dark, indecisive, confused or even lost,

There is nothing the Tarot cannot know, for it is the same as us and we are the same as the Universe which we inhabit. We are a part of and connected to all things at all times and the Tarot is a means by which we can find out where in the matrix of life we are. Let us now then take the first steps on our quest.

CHAPTER 1 – UNFOLDING THE MAP

As we unfold the map of the Minor Arcana we are presented with a multi-dimensional layout of ourselves and lives. In this Chapter we will take an overview of the map and examine in a little more depth what the map contains, before we dissect it, into card size pieces.

As a way into this we can first examine some of the differences between the Minor and Major Arcana. Devoted readers will have already consumed Volume 2 of these works and be aware of the higher, Universal or transpersonal level to which the energies of these cards apply themselves. As these are distilled or fragmented into smaller particles so they enter the individual, human or earthly level and the realm of the Minor Arcana.

Here they are further divided or categorised into the four levels or layers that comprise the human being, from an elemental viewpoint. These were shown in the Introduction, with the suit to which they belong and their elemental association. There are a great many categories to which these associations can be extended and these are helpful to learn basic information about the cards and gain an understanding of them.

As with the ancient, primal forces of nature that the four Elements are we can see them as equating to the four levels of the human being, these being the physical, emotional, mental and spiritual, as follows our little chart in the Introduction, These are mentioned here as it is important to see these as each having, or rather vibrating to, its own distinct energy pattern. When we work with the cards at this energetic and therapeutic level, we can come to see how the Minor Arcana can act as a dissection of our beings and a map of the human energy system.

This needs to be combined with an exploration of the energy of the numbers and of the four types of 'court' cards within the Minor Arcana, which we will come to next. For now we will explore these four basic energies and levels as we begin to orient ourselves around this enchanting map as have now unfolded.

We should also mention at this stage that it is important not to under estimate the importance of the Minor Arcana cards. Some Tarot readers have a tendency to belittle or even discard them altogether, seeing them as the small and insignificant details next to their 'grown-up' counterparts, the Major Arcana. However with the holistic approach we take with Tarot Therapy it is vital that we see them as equal parts of the whole, amounting to something greater than the sum of these parts, just as is the nature and construction of the human being and indeed the wider Universe. The two are intrinsically and energetically linked and cannot be separated, just the same as the ice cream cannot be whole without the cone, the lamb without the mint sauce or the chips without the fish – of course you can do this, but it is much better if you don't!

We can see the Major Arcana as the higher or inner self and life and the Minor as the lower and outer. They are both equal, and 'complementary opposite' to paraphrase a maxim I stole from Dion Fortune some books ago! The Major Arcana tells us about that which causes change, the Minor the change itself. As such the meanings of the cards are less abstract than those of the Major, but no less powerful; indeed in many cases they can be more so, since their energy can be experienced in a more direct and daily way. We can see the Minor Arcana as the lifeblood and internal organs of the Tarot, the Major the body and being itself.

In considering the suit of the Minor Arcana from a therapeutic standpoint, they are best seen in the context of energies and as such, as manifestations of their particular Elemental frequencies or manifestations. In short we see the suit cards as Elements. As we have seen in previous volumes, these Elements are the building blocks of everything we have and are in our manifest world. It is essential that we steep ourselves in the knowledge and understanding of the energies of the Elements to come to a thorough application of them in our readings. Hopefully, this book will aid that process.

Continuing our process of categorisation of the suits and Elements, we can also group them in two equal and opposite forces, or energies. These are Fire with Air, as the outer, active, dynamic, yang principle and Earth with Water as the inner, passive, inert and inner principle. This follows the ancient principle of white and black, good and evil, and so on, as it is encapsulated in the 'yin yang' symbol which demonstrates that there is a spark of each within the other. Once those equal and opposite forces are combined, just as with the holistic model, we find that there is a unified force that is greater than the combination of the four elemental energies. This brings us back to the Major Arcana.

Although we have seen the need here for the suits to be seen as elemental energies, we can also make use of the symbol associated to the suits to help in our understanding of them. Whilst the names given to these and therefore the objects themselves can vary, we will use here those that are most commonly given. These largely originated with the Order of the Golden Dawn and in particular the work of A.E.Waite, creator of the infamous Rider Waite Tarot deck. Rather than repeat them here, please turn back to the Introduction to see which symbol belongs to which suit.

Let us now take a deeper look at the contents of our map and see the terrain we must traverse on our journey. As we will see there are areas of rocky adventure, seas to sail, flights to book and desert heat to endure.

We will begin however with our feet planted firmly on the ground. The realm of the Earth provides a solid foundation for the beginning of our journey through the country we call the Minor Arcana. Here it is vital that we establish good roots, from which we can grow as we explore the other elemental realms ahead of us,

The Element of Earth relates to the suit usually in common Tarot parlance as Pentacles. This is a five pointed star, each point directing us to one of the Elements, the fifth being the unity of them in Spirit. This is usually surrounded by a circle linking the points together, making it the pentagram. These are symbols of the world, the realm which we inhabit and orient ourselves within. As we shall see in subsequent chapters, the cards and energies of this suit concern themselves with and depict those worldly matters such as our physical body and its needs and condition, as well as the ways and means by which we do this. This includes all things of a physical and financial nature. As another Tarot author put it, if you can see it and point to it, then it comes under Pentacles.

In Tarot Therapy we are more concerned with the inner energy than the outer manifestation of course. These energies are most readily and primarily experienced at the physical level. It is here that we can determine something of the energetic condition of our client at the time of a reading. It should be made clear that this is not by way of a medical diagnosis, as this is something the Tarot reader, in whatever guise, should never do as they are not qualified to do so. Rather it is more by way of an intuitive analysis, such has been demonstrated to great effect by the work of Carolyn Myss (see Bibliography). Of course one of the benefits of this use of the Tarot is that we can pre-empt physical maladies occurring, since the energetic usually precedes the physical. It follows then that by assessing the client's energetic condition at the time of the consultation and working with them to respond appropriately to whatever is found, the client can be helped to avoid the manifestation at a physical level of whatever it is that threatens to 'make them ill'.

However, back to rocks, stones, tunnels and caves of this suit. It begins deep within the Earth in some dark tunnel at the back of a cave, perhaps to which the sun only reaches at winter solstice, the time of the rebirth of the light. This may be quite apt since this suit is known as the preserver of knowledge and guardian of tradition. It contains the potential for growth, like a seed and indeed like the human being. It preserves the energy of those secrets until the time is right, when it is then released to stimulate that growth. Like this suit, it is very practical.

This suit can be labelled as the 'magic of nature', just as much as it can be about money, business and all things material. Be aware though that just because you may have Pentacles cards in your reading, it does not mean that you will be getting more and more money, wealth and gain generally. Remember that 'money is the root of all evil' and there are many instances of disasters occurring because of money, more so in recent times. In this sense, we can just equate these cards to everyday, ordinary life.

This does not mean we should see them as in anyway unpleasant or trivial. Whilst it is true we can be 'treated like dirt' and the Earth is indeed beneath us, it is vital that we recognise that we need that solidity and stability. Like all the elements, if we remove one of them from our being, we cannot survive. The Earth, depending on your viewpoint, is God's creation or a living and breathing Goddess. We always have a need for 'grounding' ourselves and 'keeping our feet on the ground'. Whatever heights we aspire to or reach, we must always at some stage, come 'down to Earth' and indeed, learn to be this way, though hopefully with the aid of our trusty Tarot Therapist, not with a bump!

The subject matter or energies of these cards gives us power to get to the centre of ourselves by means of physical and practical experience and the mastery of circumstance. Once this is achieved we can shift our focus to a faster or higher level of vibration, which is the realm of our feelings and emotions, the province of the suit of Cups. Let's get wet!

In this suit we enter the realm of Water, the often turbulent pool of our emotions and feelings. So often it is we are prey to how we feel. People tell us to 'follow our heart', little realising that for some people the tidal force of their feelings threatens to swallow them up and consume them, drowning them at once in the emotion of the moment. The challenge with the energies of this suit is to become a fully alive, feeling human being but one that is not prey to these forces. Rather we become able to allow ourselves to feel what we feel deeply and fully without threat of the emotion controlling us. By doing so we are able to flow with the force of our feelings, letting this become a trusted guide to what we want to do, but not swaying this way and then that.

The cards of this suit then inform us about ourselves at the energetic level of our feelings and emotions and the field of our relationships in general, how we relate to others and the impact this has on us. This can extend to our creative ability and some view this area as the level of the unconscious. Certainly they guide us on our journey as we search for union with our higher self. These cards depict reflection, quiet experience, love and friendship, joy and fantasy, empathy and sympathy.

The Cups in these cards are said to contain the noble liquid that lets us overcome our inhibitions against showing our feelings. They show us the necessity of recognising our feelings and allowing them to flow through us just as a river continually flows, or becomes poisoned as it stagnates. Some people can be seen or labelled as unemotional or cold. However, everyone that is alive has feelings, it is a matter of how connected we are to them and which is in control, them or us. In this way we need also to be aware of the destructive power of our emotions.

As we have seen in previous volumes, the nature of energy is to flow. If we suppress it at any level, as here with suppressing our emotions, then the energy stagnates. If we deny or pretend we are not feeling what we are, this causes a disruption or blockage in the flow of energy. This energy, like water, looks for the nearest, easiest passage to flow, because that is what it does, that is it's nature and it's molecular make up. If we do not recognise, acknowledge and respond to our feelings, they take the nearest exit – our bodies, making us ill. Emotions in this sense are never destructive of themselves, only our response to them can be, or lack of. So it is these cards can offer us tremendous, powerful and valuable means by which we can come to understand and process our feelings.

These energies are the province of love and compassion and we can see that it flows, like our intuitive ability, which is a feeling sense, not a mental one. Intuition has been defined as a download of information that translates to imagery. Our use of and response to it, determines whether we become 'bitter or better'. These energies, which are really stronger or more fundamental to our being and existence, require of us that we come to understand them and our best response is to learn to flow with them.

We can also come to understand the place, meaning and purpose of our feelings more by understanding the nature of water. Water gives life to the seed, causing it to grow. It feeds and unites us, just as rivers flow to the sea. Water is formless and as such signifies the love in our soul. These energies ultimately bring healing and plenty and create new life. The cups are at their best ones of culmination and completion, the human being feelings things fully. We can say that they give power to the mature spirit who has drunk of their wisdom and come to the awareness of another reality. One easy way to think of these cards is that they ask the question 'why', when they appear. The best way to do that is to take a deep breath, then go for it,

Asking the question why is of course the province of the mental level of our being and it to this we now focus, as we inhale deeply of the fresh air that gives this energy its form. The suit and energy of Swords based around the energy of the Element Air governs the mind and all things to do with communication. When considered, there are many forms of communication, including the spoken or written word, signs and symbols as well as all forms of travel. We must include all levels of the power of the mind here, including the ability to judge and reason, the force of the intellect and opinions and attitudes. Here we include wisdom, conflict in the mind and simple, hard facts.

We should also bear in mind that the Swords used in the Tarot are double-edged, having a sharp side for attack and a blunt edge for defence, rather like the way we tend to use words. Like Jesus used his words when he said 'I have come to bring a Sword, not peace'

Many people consider and depict Swords as the negative suit of the deck and that the cards have bad portents, their appearance in a reading bringing bad news. We should be careful in the therapeutic approach not to be drawn into this view however. As with all things, there is good and bad within. The task of the Tarot Therapist is to offer the choices and options available to the client, the Tarot excelling in depicting likely outcomes. In this way the client is empowered and armoured with protection against the swoop of the sword, should it be necessary.

In considering the nature of Air we can come to understand the energies we deal with here. Like energy itself, Air is always moving and never resting. It can be a welcome cooling breeze or a raging, destructive hurricane or whirlwind. This can be much like our minds. When we first wake or are relaxed or even in meditation, our minds are calm like an off shore breeze but when we lose control in our temper, give way to unguided and uncontrolled thoughts we speak without thought and consideration, the result of which is usually destruction and regret, just like the strongest gale or hurricane.

Either way, we can see that the energies of Swords can disperse the stagnant energy that creates tension or conflict. These energies can make the client unsettled, confused and disorientated whilst they are processed yet they can bring a peace that passes all understanding once resolution is found. We can see the Swords as the dispeller of illusion, bringing light to darkness. In summary we can call them the energies of understanding

Once we have achieved that understanding we rise up through our elemental journey to the realm of Fire. This is the province of our inner selves, the force of our motivation, drive and ambition; that which we get up for in the morning, or not as the case may be!

The force of fire within us can point to our stamina and enthusiasm. This is not a physical stamina but more of an ability to see things through, to keep going despite hardships and set-backs. Many people assert that they are being tested when undergoing such 'trials and tribulations'. However I would assert that this is not the case, rather they are opportunities to grow, learn and develop. The Universe is not an emotional being; it does not care in a human, feeling sense. It exists of energy and force, perhaps as the vehicle for some celestial being that does love us and care, but its method is to offer us chance to grow, face our failures, and admit our weakness and in so doing gain strength. This is the province of fire, that inner quality that sorts the wheat from the chaff. Admittedly the better analogy may be to find needles amongst haystacks, but the gold is there to be found (I seem to be mixing metaphors here but gold equates to fire, so I'm allowed!)

The more we learn the tougher the lessons can be, but the more rarefied, the more pure and the more authentic we become, just like the process of alchemy, which many medieval mystics pursued by way of fanning their own particular flames. So we can also relate this suit to our levels of belief, hope and trust. Not a belief in a religious sense, but a knowing within that all will be well, that we have what it takes to win out and succeed in our personal journey, whatever form this takes. So it is the energies of the suit of Rods equate to struggle and optimism, the spirit of adventure and giving rise to the creative urge. In short they challenge and show us whether we are in our power or not and how we are using and responding to this force.

So we can see that these energies bring us the 'divine spark' within that all living beings are entrusted with. It is the force that gives our bodies life, what wakes us up in the morning or simply the energy of existence. We can walk over fire when we focus its energy, we dance around it to celebrate, we tell stories by it to teach, learn and enjoy. It is the primal stuff of life, just as are all the Elements in their raw form. When we are 'fired up' we are motivated strongly, or 'on fire' when we excel at something or if we lose motivation our spark or fire is said to have gone out. The force and heat, or simply energy of fire is continually moving upwards, always looking to progress, just like human nature given the opportunity. We cannot allow this to burn unattended however as a fire left will soon consume and destroy.

The Fire we speak of can be called the Fire of Realisation and is like the kundalini force in Yoga. This is represented by a coiled serpent, said to lie at the base of the spine. Working through the study and practice of yoga can allow the serpent to rise - the force of the kundalini to be unleashed. Yogis will tell you also that this must be done in a considered and controlled manner lest the serpent effectively seize control and consume you, the fire in this case creating a lack of control which can result in physical and mental distortion. Done correctly however, the result is enlightenment. The equivalent of this force in the Tarot is seen as the rods, especially when they are shown as burning, the divine flame that has the ability to turn nothing into something. So it is we can see that through the energy of these cards, in combination with worldly experience, as given and learnt from the previous elements and suits, we can become instruments for pure, divine intervention.

Just as with each of the Elements we must learn to feed the fire carefully and steadily. None of the Elements function by themselves, they each need the other to be complete, again just as with the human being. As we journey through each of the elements, through the various experiences we create and encounter in our lives so we learn and grow from them and gradually assimilate these to become a more complete, more authentic, more whole human being. As we do this at a human level so we find ourselves moving through the greater journey as depicted in the Major Arcana. The one blends with and indeed is part of the other.

These four energies and levels of ourselves are the landscape of our map, the four corners of the globe of our lives and beings. Now we must find a vehicle by which to travel through this enchanted elemental country. We have unfolded our map and now we must plot a route to follow.

CHAPTER 2 – ORIENTEERING

As we lay out the map before us, we can see that the route before us is a case, like all good, traditional journeys, of going from A to B. However, as this journey is about following the principle of being an individual and as we like to do things a little differently, we will go from 1 to 2. Having done that, we will be so bold as to go from 2 to 3 and even then extend still further and journey on to 4. Now we have a taste for it, let us indeed keep on going until we get to 10, the final stop on our destination – for now at least.

In plotting our route we will follow an old science, something in fact that the new physicists amongst us would have us believe is as old as the Universe itself, that of Numbers, or more correctly, the science or study of Numbers. In doing this we are concerned here with the power, force or more correctly and scientifically, the energy of each Number from 1 to 10.

There are many ways of utilising the science of numbers but for our purposes here, we will restrict ourselves to an examination of their energetic value. In addition to this, and as a means of offering additional knowledge with which to arm ourselves, we will also plot on our map the colour, shape and other attributes associated with each number. Astute readers will, if you have followed all volumes of this series to the bitter end, already be familiar in part with this introduction to the numbers from Volume 1. What is given here develops these ideas further and adds to your understanding of the landscape through which you are travelling in greater detail.

So we take our first steps on the journey now and, just as we should, we will start at the very beginning, that indeed being as the lady said, a very good place to start! This of course, is with the number One. In the Tarot this is more commonly known as the Ace, but whatever word we use, it is still the start, beginning, idea or essence of something. That something, as we will soon see, depends on the suit or Element to which it belongs. The best way to view and form an understanding of the energy of One is that it represents the energy or primal force of the Element itself, akin to one drop of water, one particle of oxygen, one grain of Earth and one spark of fire. Of itself it can do little and will remain just as it is. However when acted upon, or responded to, it immediately finds a form, bringing it to the second force in the Universe, expressed as two. As such, it is known as the 'Universal Monad' a monad being a fundamental singular entity.

The number one then, brings identity to the self, but can go no further, Symbolically it represents the human will and offers us the statement 'I am', the 'I' here being of course akin to the digit 1. This energy is able to make manifest what is unmanifest, at whatever elemental level it operates on; it has the power to make real what is unreal. In this respect One represents positive action and the onus of the human being. Its shape is therefore the circle, showing us the inherent potential it possesses and offers in its continuous and unbroken line,

In human character people experiencing the energy of the One are likely to have a drive to move forward, to take the lead and follow a pioneering spirit. They will experience a need for independence and to follow their own urges and drives, influenced by this alone and not others. There will be a need to be in control and great displays of enthusiasm and energy itself can be witnessed. Optimism and self-belief can be in abundance but this can be prone to an instant inversion if an idea is not thought through or responded to; it needs something to attach itself to, whether this is another person responding or the individual itself responding in some way. Like the newly lit fire, this energy needs to be fed or it can simply fizzle out.

We can then see the One as the first stage in the evolution of prime matter, that stuff from which the Universe is made and of which we too are a part of. In this they are root of the power of the element and contain its magical seed, or simply its energy.

Once this meets with another force of energy, following the rule that 'for every action there is an equal and opposite reaction' we come to the energy of Two. This is the force best expressed as duality and balance. This happens when we add one force to another or we observe the reaction between them. We have explored this idea in the theory of complementary opposites elsewhere and I refer you to Volume 1 if you have been so lack as not to have read that yet!

The experience of Two is perhaps predictably, through partnerships and relationships. This is not just as we tend to immediately suppose, in a romantic sense but in all ways and at all levels, such as with parents, friends, in business, to bosses, employers, team-mates in sports, siblings and with children. As a positive response to this, the energy of two brings forth a certain tact and diplomacy and understanding and awareness of the existence and hopefully the needs of others, suggesting perhaps that this can be a key to many successful relationships. When working with this energy people can develop an expression of others ideas and display a hitherto unseen patience, There can be a focus on the family and home life and an almost devoted loyalty can set in, There is a need for discrimination also and like many things with a delicate balance within them, this energy can easily be manipulated by an external force with not so balanced a power.

The number two is shown diagrammatically as a single line, travelling in two different directions throughout the infinity of space, i.e. two endless lines. Perhaps this says something about those relationships mentioned above, but perhaps it is also that those two lines are destined to meet again, somewhere, at some far point in our Universe. So it is the energy of two is seen as the energy of reason and the balance inherent in the number. As the response to the energy of one it contains initial understanding and brings a sense of purpose.

As we know, one plus two equals three. This complicated mathematical equation is given in order to illustrate the progression between the balance of the energy of two and the natural result of the combination of its twin or opposing forces, the third principle, which is equated with creation and the creative impulse generally. Thus it is the tangible result of ideas and action that result from them.

Not surprisingly, the shape associated with Three is the triangle. This is seen as being formed of three elements, the one left out being Air, which apparently creates discord. Perhaps this is a contributory reason why so many Tarot authors have depicted Swords, the suit based on the Element Air as the 'negative' suit and give interpretations of the Swords cards that bring destruction, loss, misery and so on. Perhaps it just says something about the nature of the human mind and our tendency to only learn when things go wrong, the mind being the level of the human being related to Air.

However, the creative energy experienced by those under the influence of Three can also yield great acts of inspiration. Creativity is to the fore obviously, but this can express itself in many ways. The triangle, sometimes in its three dimensional form of the pyramid is often utilised in healing, to produce a focal point through which the energy one wishes to create for the patient.

As such we can see Three as the energy that gives rise to the conception and manifestation of ideas. Often an external force is needed to manifest the idea, usually in the form of another person. Three energy can give rise to an impatience or recklessness, such is the strength of the urge within experienced at this time. However the cheerful disposition and plain luck that is presents tends to see us through without disaster. Three people can have a tendency however to lack stability and do not stop to look over their shoulder to see the sometimes chaotic results of their energy.

That stability is the province of the four, the return to the state of balance experienced when under the influence of our next number. This is the number for foundation and grounding, the level platform from which we can build, safely and securely. Stability and maintaining the status quo are the watchwords adhered to here, establishing a security that will last. This is the number for Earth and for functioning correctly in society - it is a worldly number and energy. Here we experience the faculty of logical thinking and the physical reality of life on Earth. This is in part because man used to think the Earth was flat and there were no other planets in existence and the boundaries of his mind lay in what he could see with the naked eye i.e. the edge of the world off which we could fall, hence the 'four corners of the world'. Perhaps obviously, the shape associated here is the square, the balanced from of the preceding triangle.

This energy gives rise to production and achievement. When working with this energy we find a determination and follow a momentum to establish and maintain order. Four people will want to test everything for security and this love of proof gives rise to a great honesty, you will always know where you stand with someone working Four energy. Following this, they can be great advisors and counsellors, valuing truth above all else. They can find positions assisting those in power and can often be the 'power behind the throne' figure in this respect, They can however resist change through fear of disruption, If you need a timetable calculating for you though, go to them! What they can sometimes lack in their dullness and imagination can be recompensed by their enjoyment of luxury and ability to generate wealth,

Change however, is as inevitable as the tides and those tides now bring us to the force of Five. This brings a necessary progression from the stability of four with an energy of disruption, whether wanted and welcomed or otherwise. This is typically experienced as an energy that comes to us from without where we are the subject of an external force. The successful adaptation to this energetic state comes in the welcoming of this energy and by allowing that energy to flow smoothly in and out of ourselves and lives.

Whilst it is a number for change this energy is also one of expression. Essentially it is the expression of the self, the sacred human being, as depicted in the shape linked here, that of the pentagram, or five-pointed star. This ancient shape has perhaps best been shown for us by Da Vinci in his image of the Vitruvian Man'. The power of the pentagram, as many true witches know, can be invoked for creation or destruction, just like the energy of Five.

This is also the case with the impact on the human character of the energy of Five, where it will produce a positive force for change by surrender or a chaotic destruction and inversion will result. This energy represents the travelling spirit within us. This can be expressed in the sense of an urge to be physically on the move or moving from one thing to another swiftly and without pause, or contemplation. Five energy creates an enthusiasm for new things, a kind of bravado that allows us to give anything a go, advised or otherwise! It produces an ability for observation and for formulating ideas into a workable whole. Communication is accented well now and sometimes too well! There can also be a need for relaxation as that energy and enthusiasm for getting on takes over.

The smooth product and result of that change is basically progression, the province and energy of Six. This is seen in Numerological circles (or should that be squares!) as the result of multiplying three by two. Three here is the creative, productive force while two blends it with itself, so we have in Six the natural result and expression of the creative energy within us added to by an 'equal and opposite' force. We could make a simile here with the way in which a musician, performer or perhaps sportsman interacts or feeds off the appreciation and warmth, or more accurately, energy, of the audience, creating a wave of expressive energy that spurs the performer or whoever on to greater feats, adding to the audiences experience and appreciation and so it goes on. That is the pleasing energy of Six as we experience it.

So we have the sense of progressive change and the accomplishment of ideals. Previous challenges set us have been met and responded to with success and a state of harmony and happiness is experienced, Six is a number for equilibrium and self-acceptance and denotes satisfaction, cooperation and self-acceptance. It can be surmised as the number for synergy, as we have seen above, the positive outcome resulting from pooling energies or blending them together. Six represents power with knowledge and understanding.

Whilst Five was the number for Earth, Six is the number for the Moon, as the planet for cyclic events and that which brings the balance of light in darkness. This is also the planet for the Goddess, with her triple faces seen as Maiden, Mother and Crone. The shape associated with Six is the hexagram, or six-pointed star, sometimes known as the healing star. This is drawn from two triangles, one pointing up, the other down (see Volume 1 in this series), again showing us the blending of 2 x 3. This shape also reflects for us the nature of 'as above, so below' and the principle of 'complementary opposites', both ideas explored elsewhere in this series, so shame upon you if you aren't familiar with them now!

When working with or under the influence of Six, we can find that we have an increase in patience and adopt a steady and steadfast approach to projects or ourselves and our lives. It is seen as a positive influence to have, with an expansive and pleasing feel. Often we find our focus turns to the home and the creation of harmony within. This is the central pilot of our life at this time, around which all else operates. Care is needed to ensure we do not become too relaxed or open, thus rendering ourselves vulnerable to those who would prey upon us, as there are always those around, looking to exploit any weakness. With Six this can result in a resentment kicking in, the flip side to that relaxed expansion and welcoming openness of the usually positive energy of Six. Of course taken to an extreme those working a Six energy can become too house-proud, treating visitors as invaders, of their personal space and energy and becoming overly fussy and clinical. Perhaps there is something of what is now labelled as 'ocd' (obsessive compulsive disorder) within the Six, but I will leave that to those concerned with such labels to figure out!

When the majority of people are asked what is their favourite number they will say it is Seven. The reason for this we are told is that seven is the mystical number of fate and destiny, so there is an underlying or unconscious pull towards it that we have. There are many reasons way seven is related to fate and destiny and the like, from the occult world we can see that the energy of seven is principal to the workings of the Universe. There are seven main planets in our Solar System, seven main chakras in our bodily energy system and more besides which testify to this and which has been described elsewhere,

The energy of seven brings with it the ability of awareness and results in changes that come from an increase in perception and understanding, such as we receive when we absorb its power to ourselves. Its energy indicates a need to start something new or different in order to avoid becoming stale. This may involve taking a risk but these are usually necessary. Regardless of any risk taken we can also rest assured that at a higher level the energy of seven serves us in that it connects us and draws us inexorably to what we are intended to do, our fate or destiny if you will. When we work with the energy of seven there is an irresistible pull towards doing that which is right for each individual at that time.

Following this principle, seven is aligned with the planet Venus in astrological terms, a planet shrouded in cloud to preserve its workings and sense of mystery. Perhaps this is why it is the planet of that most mysterious of all things, love! The seven pointed star or heptagram gives shape or form to its energy and the colour of violet is linked to it, this frequency bringing with it an increased or heightened perception, as we have already seen.

More humanly, seven carries the energy of the intuitive person. It was an ancient belief that not all knowledge came from the intellectual mind – it was held that a 'knack' was required for some knowledge to be gained in the individual, which is now known as intuition. Previously it has been called 'Gnosis' and this gave rise to the Gnostic movement. Due to this we often find that people aligned to the energy of Seven are mystics, poets, philosophers and the like, as well as being creative souls generally. Thinking, of whatever kind, is high on their agenda and seven people often display a certain detachment from the rest of the world. They are usually of an introspective disposition and concerned with the 'things of the Universe' as we could term them. There is an awareness of a conscious connection to the Universe, to other worlds, higher powers and so on. This is what can give rise to the sense of detachment which can easily express itself as loneliness within them. In short they are the epitome of the tortured artist or mad genius, the archetypal 'mad professor' figure, so often depicted.

Now that we have aligned ourselves with our destiny we can move forward on our numerical scale and embrace the energy of Eight. This brings with it the qualities of understanding of the self, open-mindedness and the ability to judge. This has the resulting expression of establishment and commitment. Old ideas are discarded now with the wisdom of experience giving the regeneration within and without that the energy and power of Eight brings at this stage of our unfoldment. Eight is essentially the number for and energy of, knowledge with awareness.

Eight is also viewed as the key number for the link between Earth and Spirit. Astrologically it is related to the planet Pluto, seen as the planet of death and regeneration. Its shape is the octagon or eight-pointed star, a symbol of the self that it is possible to draw with one continuous line. The colour linked vibrationally to this colour is silver.

Under the influence of Eight we find a need to reconsider, to step back in retreat and objectively view who and what we are in order to ripen and regenerate. The perfect analogy here comes from astute readers will know by now as my favourite source of quotes, good old Star Trek. Aficionados will know by now with my use of the term 'regeneration' that I talk of the Borg, who have a need to periodically 'regenerate' and awake armed and ready with the knowledge and ability to go about their business and fulfil the tasks required of them.

So it is that those expressing the character and energy of Eight make excellent leaders and organisers, directors and managers. Not only are they capable of much hard work they can also visualise the purpose of it as they go. They possess a strong sense of justice and a heightened self-knowledge. They can be single-minded to the point that they can blame others for their own faults. That said they are driven enough to usually succeed in what they do. There can be a strong psychic sense and ability with this energy, stemming from this increased self-awareness and perception.

This increased level of awareness results in the culmination of the numerical path we have outlined, finding its expression in the completion and fulfilment of the energy of Nine. This energy is the expression of the maximum that is able to be achieved in any situation, before moving on to a higher level. It is the attainment of a goal and finding one's real values. Nine shows us the true path to quality of life and contentment. Nine is seen as the number representing Spirit in communication with the Earth plane, perhaps as the expression of 3 multiplied by three, where three is the creative and generative principle.

Astrologically Nine 'belongs' to both the planets Mars and Neptune as the planets of curiosity and understanding. Its shape is the 'enneagram' which is based on three interlocking triangles, symbolising the balance of different forces. The colour here is Gold.

As we learn to integrate the energy of Nine to ourselves so we absorb the qualities of understanding that comes before or perhaps beyond words. This is rather like the biblical 'peace that passes all understanding'. We can't explain it or even express it in words, it is just there. This is essentially the quality and energy of Nine. So as we learn this we become visionaries. We can now understand the cyclic nature of all things and the Universe and learn to operate with an inherent balance and will that ensures that anything we do does not upset the order of the Universe. Put another way, we learn to be and live in a fulfilled way. This can bring with it the urge to travel that stems from an inner drive to learn that quite literally drives us on.

There can be a belief that what we now know is right for all, the danger of the ego being always prevalent in the human being. This can result in a self-destructive element, which all great masters seem to have! At this stage the balance is powerful, but delicate. It is rather like the highly trained athlete - the body is capable of amazing feats of power, skill, endurance and speed yet for all that it takes only a slight strain or sprain and the whole lot goes!

However if we can succeed with the integration of this rarefied energy, we reach the beginning of a new stage, as we open to the energy of Ten. Here the end of a cycle has been reached and we prepare for dissolution and disintegration that is the progression from 1 to 0 in this number. This is the energy of collapse that is necessary before we can begin anew, like death and rebirth. Thus Ten is really energy waiting to be released. It is a completed force, neither negative nor positive, perhaps best seen as possessing both these powers and potentials.

Renewal is a concept closely linked to Ten, showing that necessary lessons have now been learnt. Here we move to a new level as we release that which we have become. The colour here is therefore White, like a blank canvas and the product of mixing the seven primary colours of the rainbow. Perhaps the easiest way of viewing Ten is as something and nothing, the ego dying to be renewed, the 1 then the 0, which is endless, like the cycle of birth, life, death and rebirth.

So it is we begin again with the energy of One, though with a renewed sense of awareness and vision. We can summarise the numerical journey on our map in the following way -

We begin by opening something up (I} which becomes polarised (2) and galvanised into action and becomes dimensional, given form and movement (3). This becomes structured and stable (4) and then moves into force (5). This force re-stabilises and progresses (6) then become highly complex and seeking (7). It reaches another level by growing (8) and finds its highest expression and fulfilment (9) before completion is experienced, whence it dissolves (10).

Now that we have familiarised ourselves with the terrain of the landscape that lies ahead of our we can introduce ourselves to the Guides we have fortunately been assigned to help us on our way and indeed show us the individual way that we need to follow for each of us on the quest.

CHAPTER 3 – THE GUIDES ON THE QUEST

There is nothing so helpful when undertaking a quest as to have a guide along to help you. As we now know, the Tarot is the ultimate guide in life and as such it does not let us down here, as it provides an abundant sixteen guides for us. These are the court cards and we will now undertake formal introductions with these and come to know them for who they truly are, as they have for a great many years been seen as mysterious and hard to know characters.

Part of the problem here is that nobody really likes the court cards, which is really very unfair on them since once you do get to know them, they are an interesting and diverse bunch, each with their own approach to and take on, life. Tarot readers however, tend to shy away from them, since they don't know if they are talking about their client or someone in their life. Clients tend not to like them since they don't know who the person they are describing coming into their life is and generally refuse to accept or admit the characteristics described in themselves.

With our therapeutic approach however, we do not have these problems. Instead we can come to know them as part of our Tarot family, each expressing a simple yet deep and powerful expression of a combination of energies. In this way they can act as guides and counsellors on our quest. They are perfectly placed to do this since they each consist of elemental forces from which we are all derived. These elements also govern the landscape on our map so they are also derived from the very same matter as that in which we live, move and have our being. The prefect guides.

Perhaps this way they are sometimes seen as a royal family, as the Court cards were once known. They have also been called honour cards, as befits their status, and perhaps less flatteringly so, face cards, for fairly obvious reasons. What is important for us to realise here, as Tarot Therapists, is that they show how the nature of the Elements move within and through the human psyche, or a least the psyche of our client in a reading, affecting what happens to them and in this way, guiding them. What we really need to achieve as we travel the Seekers Quest is a balance of all the different elements and characteristics.

So, let us introduce ourselves to these noble folk. First the Pages, as they are commonly known, or sometimes the Princess, the fair maiden or daughter of our modern, 'nuclear' family unit, as we were once laughingly called. They represent the movement of energy into form so can be seen as quite a pure force in operation in our lives. This relates to the Element of Earth and the experience of sensation and shows us the way in which things are perceived. This in turn relates to the elemental season of Winter.

As the Element of Earth, Pages are the evolutionary force of change and stand for long-term plans, just as the earth gradually and patiently shapes itself. So they are full of a steadfast enthusiasm as they set out on their quest to conquer the world. They are idealists but their enthusiasm and zest for life means they are a delight to be with. There can be a lack of maturity in their expression but it is no less pure because of this. So it is they are the perfect Valet as they have been historically depicted, the perfect Jeeves to our questing Wooster!

As beings of Earth, the Pages show us the way in which we perceive and experience things at a physical level. Their energy is primarily physical one that as it comes to us can impact on our bodies and influence what we are motivated and prone to do. In short the energy of the Pages, or more correctly Earth, informs and provokes us to what we should be doing; they help us shift this energy into a practical form. Earth energy is the slowest and lowest of the four levels of vibration we experience and this is why it helps us translate these inner forces into outer action.

If we are lacking in direction we can work with the Page/Earth energy to tap into a force that can galvanise us. If we know what we want to do but lack focus or direction again they can help us. If we have the potential and inspiration within us but not the action to back it up, our friend the Page can help.

So in the course of Tarot Therapy we see the court cards not as people but as energies, just as we do each and every card. The Pages keep us grounded and acting, doing something with ourselves and lives rather than wallowing or stagnating. Of course how each of the Court cards may manifest in our, or our client's lives may be through a person who fits the traditional description of the Page, but with the therapeutic approach we are concerned only with the inner energy, not the outer action as this is where the power to truly help and create shifts lies.

Just as we saw our unfortunate Page as Jeeves, so indeed we could come to see the next of our guides, the Knight, as Wooster himself, though this might be stretching the character somewhat! This is the son in our family, the primal energy of the element of Fire. They show us the quality of Intuition and demonstrate the strength and weaknesses of their particular Element. In the seasonal round we are in Summer now, when our plans grow and take shape.

The Knight is a force for revolutionary change, viewing change as a good thing since it brings them closer to replacing the King, which is always their ultimate aim. So it is they bring an impatient, driving energy and stand for revolution and the alternative. The Knights learn through their adventures and so make a perfect guide on the quest in this respect, for they will never quit. In this they symbolise the ego and the development of the human soul, driven by some force within to seek wholeness or completion. So it is they are the Cavalier of old, the mediaeval horsemen, noble and distinctive but not to be got in the way of.

So we see the Knights as the embodiment of the energy of Fire. In this they can bring us energy beyond imagining, power, force and the means to create, as well of course, to destroy. As we learn to work with the energy of Fire we find that our inner drive, our ambition can rise and become an unstoppable force. Of course we must learn to temper and fuel our fire wisely or we will soon become, literally, burnt out, How we do that can be taught by other Guides on our quest, for it is fact quite rare for them to work alone and we find that they seem to have a quite magical ability of appearing just as the right time, when we need that kind of knowledge, that kind of energy.

The Knights then provide us companionship on our quest as we come to terms with different aspects of our character. There is an inherent, natural knowledge that they offer us and as we learn to absorb this so we learn to tap into our own inner resources, wisdom and fire. The Knights will always respond to a sincere and respectful call for help, shining armour or not, so if you are down, lift yourself with a little Fire!

24

Now it is time to curtsy as we are introduced to Mum, the Queen. This is the emergence of form into energy, the energy of feeling and emotion where we absorb the ability to channel the power of the element Water, which they express. This is the coming of the autumn when the rains fall.

The Queen brings an energy of conservation with the good of all at heart. However, there can be a ruthlessness if she feels threatened or attacked, that can be quite sharp. Change is therefore brought slowly and carefully by this energy, to allow time for everyone to adapt to it. The Queen energy is expressed in what is often called feminine wisdom, or female intuition. In this sense it is the energy of the soul and the winds of Autumn that scatter the seeds.

The element and energy of Water is represented by the Queens, coming to us in our feelings and emotions. It is important that we do not allow ourselves to drown in the depths of our feelings and be swayed by every movement of our emotional tides and turns, which if we overdose on Queen/Water energy, we can be at risk of. However, if you feel in need of a little mothering for any reason, then she is your woman!

One of the many valuable lessons the Queens bring us in how to cope with and best respond to what we are feeling. This does not imply they are weak, feeble beings as they are of an emotional basis, but what we can learn from them is an inner strength that allows us to detach from, observe and respond wisely to what we are feeling, taking them into account as a valuable aspect of our whole being, but not the most powerful or one that we must take our direction from. It may have been that prior to meeting the Queen we would have been lacking an emotional stability but this is what their energy offers us and what we would do well to accept.

Lastly we must bow, before the King himself. This is the father who shows us the stability we need now in our process of wholeness. This is expressed through the element of Air that refreshes and clears the mind, like the deep and full breath. This is often seen in authority figures and so we come to see the King as the guardian of their particular element.

This guide shows us the wisdom that comes from their long years on the quest. They may be trying to hold on to their power and position for as long as they are able but there is no substitute for the wisdom that comes with their maturity. There can be a tendency to resist change and new experimentation now, for change tends to be seen as potentially disruptive and a harbinger of doom. The King is at the top and therefore the only way forward is down, so he wishes to stay where he is. He is like the winter, when everything seems to slow down and many things hibernate.

So the Kings bring us the energy of Air. They breeze into our lives like the proverbial breath of fresh air and bring new clarity of mind and vision in so doing. They can father us, take care of us and show us the route to what we already know within, our natural wisdom and the means by which we can follow our own Tao, or way.

The King/Air energy teaches us about our thinking and the way in which this impacts upon our overall well-being. We have a need to listen to our thoughts and learn to use our minds, but in an appropriate and positive manner. So easily we can slip into negativity and thinking that is influenced by a fearful heart and feeling. The Kings know all this and are masters at it and so it is their pleasure to educate and guide us to what they know and naturally do.

The Kings have both insight and authority and have travelled far and wide on this landscape of our quest which we call life. Now they have nothing to prove and choose instead to guide and serve others. Avail yourself at every opportunity of what they offer for they know much which we do not, however far advanced or wonderful you think you might be! If the Kings are the guardian of their particular element then it is humbling to think they have chosen us to share of what they know, so bow politely, listen and receive. They will show us each how we can become whole.

So it is we come to see the necessity of each and every one of our guides, each offering, teaching and showing us something that we need. Our task as we follow our quest is to blend a perfectly balanced alchemical mix of these raw materials, elements or energies to produce the rounded, balanced and equally proportioned character, ready to fulfil the Quest, known as The Fool, as we know.

These guides exist each to show us their individual human and elemental characteristics and it is our task to take each according to their needs to create the unique and complete individual we all are.

What we now need to realise and learn is that each of our guides are not only one energy but a combination of two, one expressed through the other. So the Pages are of Earth and this is modified by which Page they are. So the Page of Wands becomes Earth of Fire and the Page of Cups Earth of Water. We will shortly go on to meet each one but it only polite that we know a little about them before we do so.

With this combination of Elements we can see that the basic, major or primal energy is that of their type first, be it Page, Knight, Queen or King. This is then shaped, modified, distilled or influenced by their suit. So really we should think about these characters as Earth of Fire, Water of Air and so on. It is in this light that we will now present ourselves to them and find out a little more about each one.

PAGES

We begin with the Pages as they will set the scene for us and are good at educating us in the way of etiquette for those yet to come. Indeed, as those of Earth this is reflective of their function, preparing the way for what is to come, doing the groundwork and laying the foundations. None more so than the Pentacles Page who is of course, Earth of Earth.

This makes his energy slow to function and sluggish at times, as if it takes all his effort to climb out of bed each morning. Once awakened however he can keep going longer than the rest of us and there is a resolute, determined quality here that is patient, steadfast and not lacking in a little courage. He knows that come what may, he will get there in the end. The energy flowing into us when this card appears gives us these qualities and abilities, all we need do is be open to and receive them, looking for them within ourselves.

Whilst that determination can be a good thing it can also surface in a stubbornness that can act in a negative way. There is a strong practicality now that we can also receive and we can develop a knack of knowing what to do and when. Time being a human and therefore earthy thing, we can also acquire an innate sense of timing, knowing not only what to do but when to do it. We can find we are not put off by setbacks and problems, instead seeming to develop a natural attitude of getting our head down, keeping going and knowing that we will get there in the end. In the proverbial race between the tortoise and the hare, Pentacles Page is most certainly the tortoise!

We may find we need to raise our level of awareness a little as this energy can be rather too Earth bound and could give way to worldly greed and the acquisition of worldly goods and principally money. The energy can be so heavy and even intense at times as to bog us down in unnecessary detail so we would do well to examine our motives when we receive this energy, ensuring there is something of a higher nature to lift us above the mire.

This can be the energy too of a serious application to life and can anchor and ground us if we are or have become prone to flights of fancy. There is an appreciation of the physical in all its forms and care should again be taken to ensure that we do not become stuck or obsessed with these things. Pleasure is grand but that is not all there is to lie.

There is usually a strong flow to our conscience when we experience this energy, since this is the seat of the soul within the body and here we become firmly attached to all things physical. This is coupled with a strong sense of responsibility and diligence, even if at times we can be slow on the pick-up and a little dull-witted. A dullard he can be but the Pentacles Page more than makes up for this with his others qualities.

The physical impulses we have now should be listened to and acted upon, once we have made our examination of the facts which this energy would have us do. The promises we make to ourselves now we can trust and so long as we ensure we do not become lazy, solid progress can be made and expected.

The nature of the next character we meet at Court is a little different of course. Though still Earthly in essential nature since he is a Page, the Cups Page will greet us with a flourish and a little dramatic flair, since his earthiness is added to with his watery emotional self, as he is Water of Earth. His nature can perhaps best be summed up by saying that he and his energy will only do or cause us to do something when it feels right.

This energy will still make us want to achieve and get on with making our mark in the world, but we will have to feel good about what we do and how we are doing it, as well as having a deep belief and emotional conviction in the nature, purpose and principles of what we are doing. This energy can help us then to connect to a sense of questioning whether what we are doing is right for us, whether we believe in it or not and if not to consider what we will do about it.

This energy can cause us to be something of a perfectionist, reflective perhaps of a sometimes sensitive and fragile nature that can find it quite hard to be in the world with its harshness and cruelty. Once that belief is removed then this energy tells us to remove ourselves too, so trust becomes an essential quality now.

There can be a tendency now to reflection and inner exploration, of looking at how we feel like we do and what we need to do about it.

This can be turned upside down of course and we need to check when experiencing this energy where our motivation for our actions comes from. If we are feeling negative for whatever reason then we need to examine if our actions fall into the same bracket and we are doomed to failure in our current endeavours because of this.

There can be a strong psychic connection that accompanies this energy, which stems from that happy knack of turning within to listen to our feelings. The sensitivity we may feel now comes from this and the more emotional side of this energy. Strong passions can also arise when we feel deeply about something and we can take action for a cause we believe in with great conviction.

This can also be an important trait to the Swords Page, since he has to know something is right before he can act upon it. Born of Earth he is a student of the ways of the mind, through his connection to the element Air, by way of his affiliation to Swords. So it is that his nature is practical but shaped by the intellectual.

As such this energy can stimulate the mind to a level it has not experienced before and learning becomes a pre-requisite to this hungry state. The acquisition of knowledge can become a pitfall however, important though it may be, but not at the expense of action. Our learned friend here will always want to know as much detail as there is to know before he acts, but once armed with these facts he has a motivation to act as well.

This energy can also stimulate us to be more aware, both inwardly and outwardly. Perceptions are highlighted and we can train this sense to not leave us as we become the marshal and guardian of our own realm though the absorption of the energy on offer here. A formidable intellect is also on offer with the energy of this card so we can also utilise this to feed our minds with knowledge, not for knowledge's sake but for greater means at our disposal – to do whatever it is that is necessary for us on our path.

The energy here can also be one that allows us to sense and feel within our bodies what is right for us to do. There can be an inner or innate knowing how to act and what to do, if we tune into our body and listen to it. This can also come in the form of knowing what foods and so on we need and our body asks for. With our heightened mental abilities we can adopt this sense to our arsenal of weaponry on our quest with relative ease.

The Swords Page offers us an energy of truth and action, as well of course as acting truthfully and honourably. Our perceptions can guide us to what is right for us as an individual when we allow this energy in to our being and so can serve as a powerful ally and guide on our quest.

Next comes the Rods Page who brings a creative streak to his practical nature. Being of fire he can be an impassioned fellow and offers us an energy that can indeed fire us up. There can be a strong urge within us now to just get on with it as we respond instinctively to the fire the Page seems to breathe into us. We must temper this with the practicality he also has of knowing how much is enough, when to act and when to rest and so on.

This energy provokes us to do something; anything, so long as there is a sense of purpose and meaning to what we do. This energy can cause us to take up causes, live out our passions and 'be the change we want to see' to quote the ever helpful Ghandi. The reason we do what we do becomes more important when this card features in our lives and readings and so it is that we can have a tendency now to only do what we truly believe in and may make adjustments to our lives to suit these newly acquired beliefs and principles.

We can act with good faith now and use the inner resources we seem to be acquiring in droves to demonstrate our nobility of cause and purpose. We can develop an energy that is impulsive in nature but this is modified by the slower moving Earth energy that makes a good combination resulting in a more measured approach to what we do. There is a strong urge to be creative and make something of worth and use to the world as a product of our lives and this noble trait is something that will serve us well on our quest.

KNIGHTS

KNIGHT of WANDS.

KNIGHT of SWORDS.

KNIGHT of CUPS.

KNIGHT of PENTACLES.

Through each of the Pages we acquire a different way of acting and being in the world as each of their energies helps us to come to know and accept who we are and what we need to be doing here in this world. Once we have sorted this, their task is then to help us begin doing it. Once that is under way we are then introduced to the Knights, who show us how we can make the most of it all.

This is because of their innate and natural drive and ambition, fuelled by the Fire to which they belong. The Knights are the achievers and motivators and when it comes to getting ahead in the world, none more so than the Pentacles Knight. Properly addressed for our purposes as Earth of Fire, the twin elemental energies of practicality and creativity make this energy one that will ensure you finish what you've started, whatever that may be.

With the power of Fire flowing through his veins this is coupled with the ability and urge to do something and make a mark in the world, to improve things a little and make a difference. He may be a little more slow to react and act than his counterparts but once he begins to move, his steely determination and sheer rugged, bloody-mindedness ensure that he will always finish what is begun. He can never be swayed from his course, discouraged, talked out of anything or persuaded otherwise than his belief dictates. This energy then ensures that we will get moving when we need to.

This energy is also one of expertise so we can utilise this energy when it comes to us for being outstanding in our field, whatever that is. The diligent quality this gives us serves to encourage us and keep us moving inexorably toward our target. We can find ourselves wanting to stick to what we know as we absorb this energy for the Knight is a traditional one, basing his truth on what is tried and tested. This is not a time for abstract philosophies but rather practical realities. Secure within himself our Knights here essentially offers us a way to get ahead, if we have the courage and strength of heart to take it.

This is a quality and energy full to overflowing in the Cups Knight with his heady blend of Fire and Water. His creative nature is here shaped and informed by water ensuring that once his belief in a project or person is activated he becomes totally devoted to his quest and achieving his goal. His loyalty is beyond question and his heart will always be true and honest, since he cannot operate in any other way.

This makes his energy an ideal one to have as a companion on whatever our individual quest may be. This energy will serve to empower and embolden us and ensure our belief does not falter and our heart fall short of the high ideals that we can find ourselves adopting with this energy.

This energy as it is absorbed can also have a very inspirational quality to it and we can find ourselves throwing great enthusiasm and passion into something we can convince ourselves will save the world, grant us untold riches, cure world starvation, ensure equal rights for all or at the very least be worth pursuing, as it surely will now.

What is perhaps most important to this noble fellow is happiness and the fulfilment of his heart and to this end he will stop at very little, although he cannot tolerate cruelty or harm of others. Although strongly motivated he also has enough wisdom to have some patience as he sets lasting happiness and contentment above all else, so if he has to wait a while, fine.

We may find ourselves being unusually socially oriented as we work with this energy for our friend the Cups Knight is a social animal and finds some of his inspiration and creative endeavour by interaction with others and sharing something of the high force of love that he has flowing through him.

With a lack of any Earth here and a possibility of getting carried away with himself there is a need for ensuring we remain grounded when this card appears for us indicating his energy is working within us now. This can also be necessary to ensure he does not get bored and lose heart, literally, in his project. We can also find we can get intense and at times overly so as he gets us fired up so we must be aware of using determination and dedication in a manner that avoids this. The high ideals we can give ourselves now and the charm he can imbue us with mean others can crave our company and candour as we seek to fulfil the high demands of the ever popular Cups Knight.

The Swords Knight is sometimes not so popular, with his propensity for truth, at whatever cost. Being a creature of Air and Fire this at times dynamic energy can give us an almost desperate need for knowledge, for truth and for fulfilling an inner urge to know everything about whatever our chosen passion might be. This can result in our pushing ourselves forward, sometimes at cost to others. With his fiery basis pushing him ever onwards the Swords Knight brings us an energy to fulfil our minds.

We need then to be selective and choosy about what we fill our minds with. In these days of ever available information at our fingertips it is all too easy to while away many hours with fruitless and often factless information that does little or nothing to the advancement of our learning and strengthening of our soul. All the Knights want to become King, which in terms of the energy we absorb when under their influence means that we want to be expert in our field and have dominion over our self and life. To do this we must select that which resonates deeply and fully with our soul and fill ourselves with this.

To be King is to be top of our particular tree and the Swords Knight offers us the potential to fulfil ourselves with knowledge and truthful principles to live by, according to our own individual principles. We may find ourselves impatient now, a little intolerant of those circumstances and people who are moving slower than us, particularly mentally. We may need to resist the urge to finish others sentences off for them or simply make mental assumptions within that we know all that someone is saying and that we cannot learn from them. A little humility is always a powerful spiritual tool.

On the plus side, the Swords Knight energy does allow us to finish what we started and to deal with difficult or challenging situations or people in our lives. Fuelled by the ego of our minds though we may be, because of the energy we receive now, our self-belief and confidence in our knowledge and dynamism to carry a project to completion means that we feel that nothing can stop us. We can act and act swiftly, wielding the Sword of Light and Truth to sweep away that which would block or slow us. Suddenly, everything can seem possible and we assert ourselves with belief and not a little courage.

The same is also true of the Rods Knight, when we have learned to focus and channel his particular energy successfully. With the double dose of fire that comes to us through him, this is not always easy. A dynamic soul he certainly is and there is a strong need to temper that fiery force flowing freely through us now. This can be a difficult one to get to grips with and master, but once done we have a seemingly inexhaustible force at our disposal.

It can be quite common when we first experience this energy to become acutely aware of all that is wrong in our world resulting in frustration as well as a degree of anger. Once we learn to focus that fuel into action we can see we have an excellent opportunity to sweep away that which is now serving us now, to get to grips with and defeat with a positive strength whatever is in our way.

However that sense of frustration can also be fraught with danger and we may find ourselves prone to losing our temper and even feeling violent or aggressive tendencies. We can allow that fiery force to give rein to this darker and lower part of our character but rather we have a need now to use that motivation to propel ourselves forward and rise above those baser drives.

This energy can also make us ready to defend what we believe to be right and to fight for its successful outcome. Motivation is not then a problem for we can access a great store within ourselves now. Indeed this can be to such an extent that like all raging fires, we need to be careful we do not burn ourselves out and extinguish ourselves by going over the top. At the very least we will experience a restlessness within which will keep simmering away. We may find a sense of unpredictability and one day leap out of bed and rush out the door to conquer our particular world.

There can be a great love of life now and enthusiasm for just about anything. A strong flow of creativity can come to us as the Rods Knight energy asserts itself. We may find ourselves with an excess of energy and need to find an outlet for this, perhaps through physical activity of some kind. This at the very least can help us ensure that we do not give way to the violence or destruction which hangs over this energy like a black smoke and instead focus on the higher ideals which also accompany the Rods Knight.

QUEENS

Following on from all that Fire we find as we come to meet the Queens we are diluted a little and allowed to quench our thirst. The Queens bring an energy that exemplifies the soft and receptive, feminine within all of us, connecting us to our hearts and our feelings with their basis of water and its qualities and energies.

So the basis for the Pentacles Queen as water is to feel her way forward and act on what she knows is right. Here we are stimulated in our heart to do what is right. Our conscience can come to the fore now and we may find that we are first alerted to what is not right in our lives at a practical level. This may lead us reassess certain aspects of our lifestyle if it is not in accordance with the deeper longings of our heart and soul.

Once we have accepted these things and release outdated and outmoded habits and ways of living we can turn our attention to what will fulfil us at this deeper level as we work this energy into our being. This can lead us to try new things, leave aside what we do not feel is good and positive for us and adopt and integrate what is. There can be a certain amount of experimentation now so it is important we are closely attuned to our soul and follow the promptings in our hearts.

We can find ourselves stimulated by the beauty around us and in our interaction with others we can find also that we cannot tolerate or relate to those who do not exude these qualities, or rather operate on a level of fear or even unexpressed anger or hate. With a heightened sensitivity as all the Queens bring to us, we will simply leave such folk aside and quietly detach ourselves from their company without causing a fuss. We may find a need to indulge ourselves with artistic and creative pursuits to express the love of beauty we feel now.

Equally though we can find ourselves unusually motivated by a sense of justice and fairness in the world and the dealings of political and civic activities as the Queens earthly energies assert themselves. We may find ourselves doing well financially and economically as we do this, finding the truth in Keats' poetic statement that 'a thing of beauty is a joy forever'. This can also be demonstrated in an increased generosity for this queens' big heart as do they all and there can certainly be as much pleasure in giving as receiving.

Should this energy not be processed in a healthy way we can find ourselves possessive and jealous as we seek a path of flattery of the ego, which can only lead to isolation and separation. However it is more usual that by this stage the beauty and love within our hearts will win through and our intuitive idea shows itself to be the stronger.

There can be a different challenge with the Cups Queen and her double dose of water. Here perhaps predictably we need to ensure we are not drowned beneath tidal waves of emotion that we can be subject to when we meet with her and her deeply soft, emotional energy and nature. Here we can care, but care too much. Anything of an emotional nature can set off streams of tears and we can be easily subject to exploitation because of this.

The soft and caring path is the way of the heart and whilst we certainly need this we also need to learn now to care for ourselves first. This is not to be selfish but to come to know that it is only when we have addressed our own needs can we truly expect to be of true, real and lasting service to others, and demonstrate our love in this way to good effect.

There is a strong empathy at work with this energy and this can be a hard quality to integrate. The world can seem a cruel and cold place as everywhere we turn it seems we find suffering ab0ut which we wish to do a lot but can usually achieve little. It is enough here to know what we feel, acknowledge our desires, do what we can and release the rest. If we do not we can risk hardness of heart and bitterness as we withdraw from the world to make it easier on ourselves.

When we allow ourselves to love ourselves just as we are, then we can find the growth and strength that this Queen knows, as our own and freely offers to all those who come to her. Remembering again that the opposite of love is fear rather than hate we may need to look at our fears and learn to love them for what they offer us and how they do in fact, serve us.

So the energy here is entirely emotional in its nature and so we are challenged to integrate our emotions as one aspect of our being, one quarter, fully and completely valid but no more than this. We can learn now not to be slave to our feelings, turned this way and that but know that each emotion tells us something and we can embrace this without it threatening to destroy us. The natural knowing and wisdom that all Queens have will show us this if we but allow it to do so.

We may need to ensure we keep ourselves grounded now and we can find that we are in demand for our empathic qualities and ability to listen and really hear what is on the minds and hearts of others. We may need to keep our tendency for idealistic goals and grandiose ideas in check as we hatch yet another plan that will cure the world of its ills! When we place love in the centre of our hearts we can know the profound truth of its power and strength too as the strongest force and energy in our world which this Queen shows, with a soft smile in our direction.

Of prime importance to the Swords Queen is the working of her intuition and she operates fully around this. This comes from her blend of air and water, the head and heart energies that in their combination give the sense of cognisance; that of knowing. When this lady is in her power and we work successfully with this energy as we receive it, we gain this powerful and valuable sense of knowing. This is a little like an alignment with the eternal Tao whereby we just seem to know instinctively what is right and correct for us to be doing and do it.

The correct balance of these energies is vital to the Queens well-being and of course to ourselves as we see her appearance in our cards, sending us her energy. Whilst the benefits of this balance should not be underestimated, it is good to check ourselves to see if we are manifesting any of the out of balance symptoms.

If there is an over reliance on the mental energies then both we and our regal friend here can become cold in our regard to others. Sharp-witted we may be but this can show itself in a harshness and sharpness of word and thought. Speaking our mind is not a problem but we may need to guard against over doing this! Ever alert we can find ourselves quickly forming opinions and making mental judgements about those we come across and just about everything in our path. We need to ensure we are not giving way to spite here and cultivate tolerance and acceptance.

Equally if the energies veer toward the heart too much we can become too soft and turn to 'people-pleasing' and display what are really known as 'passive-aggressive' behaviour patterns. We can become too much of a walk-over and be exploited by those with mind to do so and eventually we find a retaliation takes place and we either lash out or shut down at the heart level, neither of which are healthy places to be living in.

Concerned however with truth and justice our Queen brings us a sense of fairness and balance both inwardly and outwardly. We can find a fluidity of movement and flow through our life with grace, rhythm and balance as we align ourselves to that Taoist place within and without.

Lastly here, we bow before the Rods Queen, perhaps a little nervously. This is due to our perhaps sensing her strength and power, which with the fire inside her soul she makes no pretence to hide. She is not unfeeling however, since her nature is a watery one and this connects her to her own heart and to those of others, for she is blessed through this combination with a great power to understand and relate to others and their struggles within.

However she can lack a little in patience and there will be a time when she will sigh and push us onwards, tired of dawdling, faint-heartedness and trembling. Like all good mothers, she can have the ability to dispense 'tough love', not suffer fools gladly and operate a cruel to be kind policy. This serves to motivate and push us a little as we absorb and work with this energy. This energy will not allow us to be idle for long and the drive we feel means we must follow the truth of our heart. Indeed our aspirations may well be high at this time as the inner fire asserts itself.

There is a strong degree of loyalty and generosity now and we find that we are comfortable with expressing our feelings, whatever these may be. We may find that some people cannot deal with this as we can be more open than can be comfortable which some will see as confrontational. However when we check the motivation in our hearts, which is all important with this Queen's energy, we can usually find a positive alignment and reason for our actions.

There is a strong urge towards the spiritual now too as those high ideals and aspirations take hold. With the strong emotional streak present too, we can find we have a need to form close bonds, links and friendships with others of like mind, namely spiritually minded. There can be an urge to seek out groups and gatherings wherein we can feel comfortable, accepted and understood. There can be an urge too to serve others due to the result of the combination of fire and water energies, showing caring for others in a spiritual sense. This can also show itself in a closeness and need to be with nature in her varying aspects. Less literally this energy causes good and positive things to grow, both in ourselves and those we choose to serve now.

KINGS

KING of WANDS

KING of SWORDS.

KING of CUPS.

KING of PENTACLES.

Service can also be a key factor with the Kings, since in principle at least, they are there to serve their subjects and their country. In this respect we are their subjects and their country as we are the recipient of their energy. Here this is air in nature and so we think of the mastery of their particular level, or suit. The acquisition of knowledge and the application of truth are the maxims they work by as we shall see as we are ushered before the throne and bow low.

First we meet the King of the world, in as much that his dominion is over the earthly realm that his title of Pentacles King alludes to. With his focus of Air coupled with Earth he is motivated by acting on the truth that he knows and is a creature of principle and he will go to great lengths to assert this. So it is with us as we receive his energy, when matters of truth and justice can become important to us.

Just as with the King being prepared to do so, we may find ourselves needing to get our hands dirty as we can become prepared to act on that truth and those principles to which we hold dear. We will find ourselves able to deal with the ways of the world now and meet any challenges of truth and justice that we may come across. Loyalty can also be an important issue for us now and we may find ourselves tested in this respect, to prove ourselves or otherwise to what we know in our minds that we should be doing.

Not necessarily prone to displays of warmth, affection and emotion, we demonstrate this by what we do as we demonstrate the maxim that 'actions speak louder than words'. As we absorb this energy we can gain great confidence, both in own abilities and our knowledge, along with the ability to carry out what we need to do to achieve our aspirations in the world.

We can also develop great patience from our understanding of the ways of the material and practical world and the struggles that we and others can sometimes face in dealing with it. We may need to ensure that this does not give way to laziness but our innate urge to assert ourselves and the sense of authority that comes to us (as it does with all the Kings) should allay this.

The Cups King is more in touch with his heart from his blend of water with air. His challenge, and ours as we are offered his energy, is to master our emotions rather than be their slave. With the elevated knowledge of the airy King also on offer however, we have a wonderful opportunity now to come to fully understand the role of our feelings and emotions. With the intuitive blend produced by air and water we can find that we are able to allow ourselves to fully experience and feel all our emotions, from the pleasant to the scary and downcast and come to know how they serve and teach us and what they are trying to tell us about ourselves in that moment or situation that has produced that feeling.

Whilst the Pentacles King may be motivated to use his body in action and perhaps exercise, the Cups King is more akin to apply knowledge and use this in relating to others. We can become expert communicators under his tutelage and find ourselves able to negotiate in even the most difficult of circumstances, becoming expert ambassadors for peace and understanding, not least with ourselves. Indeed, with this energy we can make massive strides forward on that most tricky of paths, that of learning to love ourselves for who and what we are. With the twin energies the Cups King brings us we can gain the all-important understanding required for this.

Keeping grounded can become something of a task as we can become prone to idealism as well as a little religious fervour and even fantasy. By using the energy of air to remain objective and honest this too can be dealt with as we come to know and love ourselves that little bit more. This can also be expressed in some creative outlet and we may find we have a good sense of what will appeal to others.

Indeed the strong and clear ability to relate to others is pushed to the fore with this energy and this can be used to great effect, not only through our diplomatic endeavours as mentioned above but also through our close and more personal acquaintances and relationships. This King does not rule alone and with his energy coursing through our veins we will usually find that we have a deep and strong desire to seek out those we can relate to and form new bonds and ties with them. Equally, those we cannot relate to may fall away from our sphere of influence and move out of our lives.

The Swords King can be quite a different kettle of fish with his dual blast of air. This makes him an air-head of course and he can live and operate as if his head is in the clouds permanently so we immediately find a principle need for grounding. If we work hard at this now then great progress can be made in terms of understanding and knowledge.

The acquisition of knowledge becomes our prime motivator when under the Swords Kings influence as he seeks to breathe more and more into his mind. It is as if this King is acutely aware that we do not use all of our brain power by any means and he seeks to do just that. We may find ourselves devouring books, books and more books now, eagerly enlisting for courses to further add to what we already know. We may find we need to avoid the trappings of ego and coming across like we know everything about everything, even if we do! Humility may not come naturally now, but this is precisely why we need serve ourselves a good helping of that particular pie.

As we advance our minds now we are offered the benefit of great insight, to ourselves and others. The workings of the world can become clear to us and can even reveal some of the mysteries of the Universe, which we may find ourselves concerned with now. This we can pass on to others for we can feel a great pull to teach and educate, passing on the important truths we have come to know and have been revealed to us from our studies.

What we may lack in practicality now we can make up for in awareness and insight and the ability we can cultivate to get to the truth of the matter. Once we know this we cannot be dissuaded by any alternative route for we can become the living exponent that 'the truth shall set you free'. Indeed we may find ourselves dealing with matters of law and authority while under the dictate of the Swords King.

We may need to guard against isolating ourselves and allowing the tendency to relate and communicate to turn in on itself. We could find then that we can give way to a more sadistic and even cruel, harsh and judgemental side to this ego driven, dominant perspective. When working with the energy of the Swords King we are well advised to undertake some breath work and perhaps meditation, both to ensure the healthy flow of air through our body, which will in turn work its magic and influence in our minds. This can also work to soften the heart and keep us in touch with our feelings as we need to now.

The wisdom of our last King, that of Rods, shows itself in a different way. His fiery energy fans the flame of his knowledge, giving him a charismatic and magnetic charge that drives him on and creates inspiration in others and ourselves as we aspire to become more like him, this being the effect he seems to have automatically.

Whilst he may well feed his mind he also uses the fire that burns within him to bring that knowledge to those around him for their own advancement and progress. His fire is something of a spiritual one and he seems to know instinctively the truth of what is right and good for all. The King here wishes to remain so and so we will find our motivation turning towards improving our lot and exerting our influence for the common good rather than just the self. We can become wise enough now to see the purpose of service and guiding and assisting others on their journey to wholeness.

A great passion can flow to us now and whilst we can be swift to act once we see what needs to be done we may need to ensure that this is not overdone or that we act too swiftly. There may be a little hot-headedness that can arise as we give way to our passions and whilst there may be a positive motivation behind this we do need to ensure we are not getting carried away. I am reminded here that the Rods King is rather like the manager of a football team, and that it is possible to both love and hate him at the same time!

Many new impulses and ideas can come to us with this energy and we can find ourselves exploring new and uncharted territory that we may not have been expected to explore prior to this. We can allow ourselves to be inspired and let out a creative juice that will be added to the beauty of the world; the good and development of others being still important to this King and his rule.

He is a born leader and we may find ourselves in a position where we need to lead but we can be assured our natural flair, charisma and ability will cause us to shine and indeed shine brightly. Others will seek to follow our lead and light and our desire to serve can protect us from the trappings of ego as we take ourselves and those with us that little closer to enlightenment and wholeness.

So now that we have familiarised ourselves with the map of our quest, observed the formalities as we should and met the guardians and guides that will accompany us, we can begin reading our map and exploring the landscape on it.

CHAPTER 4 – THE QUEST

Now, at last, we can unfold our metaphorical map, lay it out before us and finally begin our Quest. Every good quest must begin somewhere and for us we start with us, the Aces, the initiatory point, where we can find an answer to the timeless question 'Who am I'?

We know already from previous volumes that we are the sum of our parts and here we undertake an examination of those parts. These are the Elemental energies, encapsulated in their essence in each of the four Aces, which illustrate for us what they are. So it is we come to know each Minor Arcana card as the combination of the elemental forces, each describing and expressing a unique aspect of the human being and of the world around us of which we are an intrinsic part. It is for this reason, as I have stated at every chance possible throughout these books, that we can come to see these underlying, causal energies that go to shape the client and what is happening in their life, when we give a Tarot consultation from a therapeutic standpoint.

Of course with their being four cards of each number, we can see immediately that each of these four cards has in common a basic or defining energy, power or expression. In Tarot Therapy this is what we understand from the number of each Minor Arcana card. Before we dissect the expression of this fundamental energy, let us first examine what it is we are dealing with in each number. I have included a brief overview of each number in this and the previous two volumes, so working on the assumption that you have absorbed these, now we can see the full landscape through which we must travel. Let us look a little deeper before we forge ahead into each section of this sacred land.

ACES

ACE of SWORDS.

ACE of WANDS.

ACE of PENTACLES

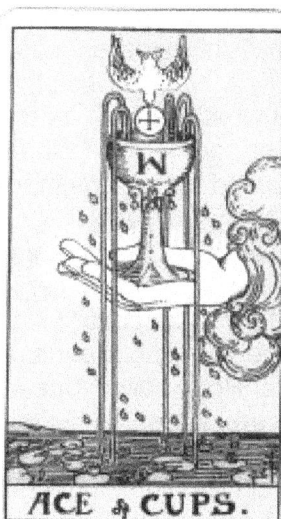

ACE of CUPS.

We have identified already that the One is the self, the I and the beginning of the process of self-awareness. What we can go on to see now is how we do this. This primal force or essence of the Element as we have previously expressed it, needs an outer showing of this inner force. This we can find in the creative impulse, the urge to be something, or more correctly, someone. This can find its expression in self-identity and more directly, confidence, Until we tap into this energy, we can become slave to the fears and insecurities that all young people face as they search for who they are. What we are is an amalgamation of Earth, Air, Fire and Water and these four cards show this truth to us, allowing us to tap into the confidence that they give us,

As with all stages of the quest, it is of vital importance that we do not shy away from and repress the flow of energy. This way lies the trap and impotence of insecurity and fear. Rather we must accept and absorb the energy we find here and determine to do something with it. Given that the nature of energy is to flow and that we are at its source here, so the urge to push on will always be there, somewhere, however deeply buried in the individual. Each and every human being is unique and original and the challenge here is to find that uniqueness; in short, to be who you are. Those not doing so are often those in denial, burying their uniqueness beneath layers of whatever may be their particular chosen opt out clause, of which there are a myriad these days from which to choose. Instead we are called upon to be innovative and confident in that.

Symbolically the One is represented by the circle, especially apt since as Ralph Waldo Emerson observed 'throughout nature this primary figure is repeated without end'. The concept of Oneness, as we are the sum of our parts, is echoed again in this circle, which Alexander Pope called 'one stupendous whole', which we most certainly are. Here the circle represents that wholeness and unity to which we must always aspire. It is said we have an instinctive pull towards circles, something many marketing agents are aware of now, and especially to their centre, since we see ourselves within them. This follows the manner of symbols to act directly upon our subconscious mind, bypassing the logical intellect of the conscious and so we can perceive that wholeness, or even perfection then we observe or perhaps meditate on, the circle.

Equally, mathematicians looked upon the circle as the source of all other shapes, akin to the female womb. The Greek term for this was 'Monad' which can be translated as 'Oneness'. The Monad was referred to variously as the essence, builder, foundation and the immutable truth and destiny, all adjectives which fit perfectly with our idea of the energies of this numerical principle.

Michael Schneider in his amazing book 'A Beginners Guide to Constructing the Universe' tells us that ancient philosophers expressed this Monad numerically as 111111111 x 111111111, which equals 12345678987654321. The meaning behind this is that all other numbers can only express other or variant qualities of, for our purposes, the energy of One. So we can see that these numerical values are energies, expressed as the unfoldment of this parent number takes place, through us.

If we multiply or divide any number by this unity principle, it remains the same (5 x 1 or 5 ÷ 1). So we can see this wholeness is within all things, aiding and abetting all it comes into contact with to find its way home again, much like us on our noble quest here. It is, as I said in Volume 1, that the Tarot is the perfect guide through life, for it contains all life. Here this is summed up on these four cards, the perfect expression of the physical, emotional, mental and spiritual energies respectively.

More scientifically we can also see that nothing can exist without a centre around which it revolves. Examples of this can be the nucleus of an atom, the Sun in our Solar System and the heart of our bodies. If either of these fail for whatever reason, the whole collapses, like the black hole in the centre of a galaxy. Hence we must avoid being 'pointless' and instead always strive to 'get the point', this being here the centre of our quest.

So much in nature operates in perfect circles and there can really be no other form of a circle but a perfect one – the only difference is in size. Observe the ripples in a pond, craters caused from objects, flowers as they bloom, the Moon at its zenith, the rings within trees and stars as they explode; each perfect expressions of Nature's unity and wholeness.

So it is we come to see that our quest is really to find that which already lies within and always has. There are but four paths we can choose, the way of the body, heart, mind and spirit. Each is a very different road and at times they intersect and even create crossroads, but each leads inexorably back to this central point from which we begin. It is here we find that central point of unity and wholeness that equals enlightenment.

Let us now take a look at the energy of each of the Aces.

The Pentacles Ace is seen as bringing a strong and positive blessing in the material world. As we know Pentacles are the stuff of Earth so here this energy can be experienced as an urge to begin something new, to start a project and take a practical step forwards. It is important that we respond to this energy in some practical and tangible way given that the nature of energy is to flow and so we must go with that flow. If left, the results here can be an unexplained sense of frustration and impatience. This can be remedied if we or the client, ask ourselves what we really want to actually do and take one measure, however small, to doing it.

The Pentacles Ace brings with it the chance of great material things, if the energy is responded to and carefully built upon to completion. Adjacent cards will tell us much about how this will need to be done for these goals to be realised. For now though, it is enough to begin. Many people think that because we are dealing with Pentacles this means money and wealth but riches can come in many forms and how these things manifest will depend on the individual and their focus and motivation in life. A large part of this can be their level of satisfaction and inner peace.

The energy of this card brings with it a desire to 'speculate to accumulate' and it can be the card of the entrepreneur. New projects beginning now are well aspected and it is important that the foundations are laid carefully and properly. It is important for the individual with this card not to rush or try to surge ahead too quickly as can be their urge from within now.

Looked at from a more spiritual viewpoint, this card can bring an approach to spirit through the things of the Earth and if this is followed to its highest potential can bring the client to a place of understanding that 'god', the Universe, Spirit etc is in all things and indeed links all things together. So this card has a pleasing energy that brings a motivation the client is well advised to consider before they act, in order to reach their highest potential.

This motivation also translates into an increased ability to endure adversity with patience and calm. As the beginning of the path to worldly success we can tap into a pure essence now that helps us deal in a positive way with whatever life throws at us. This enables us to live life rather than survive it.

Our instincts may be heightened now and if we tune into our body it will tell us what we need and what is good and otherwise for us. Labour and work in the world will be justly rewarded and the client should be encouraged to use their creative energy in concerted effort. This card is like a seed that properly planted and cared for, will grow and flourish into something full of life, health and vigour.

In traditional Tarot interpretations the Ace of Cups is often seen as the beginning of a new love or relationship or can indicate a birth. When we look to the inner energy of this card what we can see is that the client may feel the pull towards a need or desire for a new relationship or to explore a connection with someone. It may be that there is a need for a new person to come into their life in some way, perhaps to inspire them or just to create a new energy in their life.

As the Ace, we are dealing with just a drop in the ocean here. This is just the potential for this new relationship, inspiration or connection to happen and it needs a response to its energy, just as is the case with all the Aces and indeed the energy of all the cards really. So this card brings with it the ingredients necessary, usually in the form of desire, attraction and inspiration, for the individual to realise the true love within their heart and the fulfilment of their emotional desires.

This energy can bring about the need for an emotional release of some kind, to release some held in tension. It may be that the client is feeling or becoming aware of a heightened sense in their emotional self and feel a deep and strong desire to express what they are feeling within. One way in which this can find a release is to find themselves in an experience of 'love at first sight' so they should be warned!

The Cups Ace represents a feminine power and energy as well as bringing an energy that is nourishing and protective. It brings what can be a strong creative urge and anything that inspires or stimulates the individual now should be expressed, in whatever way is best for them. Ideas can come thick and fast now. Cups are about our emotional selves as we know so here we begin to explore our faculty of feeling. Given that the Ace is the seed and we are concerned with matters of life, at least in part, this card can bring a literal seed, in the sense of conception. This may be literally or the conception of an idea or project.

The individual may well feel a pull towards beginning to follow a path that is concerned with their emotional happiness. They may seek new understanding, of themselves and their loved ones and can often have profound insights and have the ability to express simple truths in a powerful way. Above all there is the need now to express whatever emotions are felt.

The client can also be told that they should ensure they do not miss any good chances or opportunities that may come their way with this card too. We do not usually experience the Aces as a slap across the face, more a subtle inclination that we need to stop and be still to feel. Courage may be needed to follow an idea through and to believe in the dream, the inspiration and its possibilities. The card can be seen as turning fantasy into reality.

The card has been called 'the illumination of the beauty of nature' and is likened to the Holy Grail, the vessel from which we receive our immortality and healing. It is rather like the spring that bursts forth from the ground or the first welcome drop of rain after a drought. Quite literally, no life can exist without it. The energy of this card brings purity and healing to the individual.

The essence or energy of the Swords Ace can be summed up as the truth that is the triumph of positive thought. This is the beginning of our thought process and how we respond to it and use it can be critical to the reality that we experience.

One of the strongest and clearest spiritual laws is that 'thoughts are things'. It was Buddha who said that we create the world by our thoughts and quite simply that 'we are what we think'. Given that with the energy of this card we are now at the beginning of our

56

thought process, now is the time of greatest opportunity and chance to create the reality that we want and choose.

This is a good time for the individual to be looking at what their thinking is and where it is taking them. It is time to look at and take control of what ideas and thoughts are coming to us. By implementing this, we can use our thoughts to produce the results that are good for us and lead us to have the life we choose.

Under the influence of this card we can look to the new, like a breath of fresh air. We can become our own champion and soon believe and feel like we can take on the world and win, as surely we can. Speaking and sticking to our truth is vital now, as the clear light of dawn will shine clearly into any falsehood or deception and show it for what it is. Especially, we must ensure we are not deceiving ourselves and the way to this is simply through honesty. Our mental powers can be employed to great use and effect now and this starts with honesty, truth and clarity.

This is a great time to be planning any new project and for paying attention to details. With the influence of this card, minds are sharp and can possess great insight and ability to see things we may miss at other times. The energy of this card can be like an impenetrable suit of armour that will deflect anything that is thrown at us. It is as if through our powers of thought we can turn fantasy into reality.

There can be a strong sense of freedom with this card, something that can be the result of free and original thinking and new, positive inspiration and ideas. Any limited or restrained thinking will produce the same in its outcome so we need this freedom of thought and originality of approach. The incisive energy we can have now gives us a real discernment and ability to see things as they truly are, without complication. Any illusion is dispelled and instead, rational thought and logical thinking come in, giving light to dark places.

This energy allows the client to confront the source of their wisdom and the sword of truth of this suit flows freely. This card brings the essence of new thinking that can lead us to achieve whatever goals we set now that are based in truth and honesty, within ourselves.

With the Rods Ace the beginning we make is more one of motivation than action. Indeed in that statement lies the crux of the energy of this card. We can feel an impulse within that pushes us on onwards and it is vital that we respond to this within us and seek a direction for it, as the danger here is that the spark that is this card can fizzle out.

This card can signify the beginnings within us of a creative endeavour or a new enterprise of some kind. This brings up deep reserves of energy within us that we can draw on as we prepare to act. The energy here can swell within, directing us to move forward on our path, whatever that might be.

As a result of this influx of new energy we can experience a heightened sense of enthusiasm. This in turn may well open up areas for progression and development in our life. Again it is important that we ensure we respond to this energy or we can find we miss out on opportunities and chances that the Universe may put our way now.

We should also be aware that any potential we may feel will remain just that without something to connect it to. This will need some consolidating force to connect to it, to ensure the energy can be turned into reality. There may be a need for a degree of patience however, for this is just the beginning. With careful fanning of the flame ignited here, we can see a steady growth, not just in energy and enthusiasm but in strength of purpose and motivation.

This card brings a rise in vitality and we can feel brave enough to be original with our ideas and approaches. As such, this card is a positive symbol of self-expression as our individual soul aligns itself with the Universe. This card is rather like a primal force of the Universe and is like that which we and all living things are made of and connected to. It is in short, the spark of life. The energy is released rather than invoked, as it rises from within us. So the energy of the card is a catalyst for the client, enabling them to come to terms with deeper issues within them.

TWOS

Just as the Aces show us the beginning, the Two, quite logically, is the next stage on, representing the principle of balance and duality. The Ace is the single, the Two the equal and opposite reflection, a little like staring at ourselves in the mirror. We can define this energy as a 'complementary opposite' force, something that reflects ourselves back to us to show us our real truth by providing that balanced reflection.

This can of course be seen as the masculine and feminine principles or polarities as well as positive and negative. When the Two's appear in a reading, the question is often whether the energies are being used in a positive or constructive manner, or in a negative and destructive one. The cards around this will give a good indication of this.

The potential of the energy of the Two is indeed, two-fold. The energy here can effectively be used for attack or defence. Done positively this power can be used to achieve an inner balance in the clients life in an active way. This means they will respond to this inner energy by taking active and positive steps to finding and implementing their own sense of balance within and without. If used for defence the Two energy can still be used to create that same balance but this time it is done in a passive way which at its worst could result in inertia and laziness.

This energy brings an impulse to achieve. It can be utilised to achieve personal gain in a worldly way and also for spiritual gain, depending on where the individual's motivation is placed. Usually the outworking of this inner energy is a state and sense of balance and peace within the client. This gives a sense of proportion and an avoidance of extremes, which in whatever way, help the person stay on the 'straight and narrow' path through their life at this time. The appearance of the Two indicates it is not a time for any extremes and is instead a time to follow that 'path of least resistance'.

The Two is an energy of agreements and negotiations and the client could be experiencing much in the way of conflict now, unless some adjustment is required within them to restore a lost balance. The client is well advised to weigh up pros and cons before taking any action now, so that when they do the act is decisive and definite and gives the result required.

Historically the number 2 was seen as representing polarity and division. The reason for this was the 1 was seen as the Divine, in whatever from and anything coming in alongside this therefore detracted from that perfect unity. So 2 can be taken as a number for division and a falling apart from union with the Divine. It is seen as possessing a contradiction and so is linked with the number for contradiction and the lesser, material world,

Geometrically it is expressed as a line, the inference here being getting from one point to another. This follows the scientific principle that for anything to manifest, there must be polarity. This is rather like the breath pattern, where in must follow out, the positive and negative poles, the opposite motivations of love and fear, the yin and yang, pressure and release, matter and anti-matter and of course the male and female.

It brings a need for harmony and mutual support, seen from the expressions of speaking with a forked tongue, being in two minds and being two-faced. Just as we give so we need to receive and strive for a balance between the head and heart or thoughts and feelings. From conflict must come cooperation and from blame, responsibility. We know that opposite poles attract and these separate forces try to unite.

In numerology, two is the only number where adding it to itself is the same as multiplying it by itself ($2 + 2 = 4$, $2 \times 2 = 4$), showing how it is really the balancing point between unity and all the other numbers.

In the Pentacles Two we enter the unpredictability of the material world. The experience of this card can be rather like walking a tightrope, where its subtle influence both causes us to try hard to maintain balance as well as it taking just a little energy to knock us flying!

We need to maintain our effort then in what we are doing when we see this card, to retain a sense of duality. This can manifest as our paying some attention and care to our career and work, perhaps needing to look in a little more detail and care than we have been. It may be that things are a little unsteady at the time this card appears but with a steady focus progress can be made. The message here is that it is about how we cope with what comes our way, on a material level at this time and we may be challenged and given an opportunity to cope better than we may have previously with our conditions.

Planning and structure may be required to best respond to the energy of this card and there is good cause to weigh up our material prospects now. Gambling and risk taking will be ill advised when dealing with the energy of this card and the importance of maintaining a sense of perspective, harmony and balance in our business affairs and working life should not be forgotten. This energy can show the cycles at work in our lives and we need to be open to their flow if we are to succeed.

Of course there is the option we can take to try and manipulate what we are dealing with and force others hands or the outcome to get what we intend. If this is the choice and path taken, great care should be exercised not to lose that sense of balance and perspective and become reckless in our approach. This energy can make the comfort and pleasures of the purely material life and its riches an attractive proposition, but as with anything under the influence of the Two, this should not be to excess. Extravagance and recklessness are two qualities and energies that are bound to bring us crashing down from that tightrope at this time!

With Pentacles predilection to draw our attention to matters of the wallet (or purse) this card or energy can come with a warning to be prudent and avoid over-spending or these days, over crediting ourselves. Care and attention are the financial watchwords now and if things are managed with an avoidance of speculation, steady progress is possible. We need to establish and maintain a level of financial stability and with the proper care and attention, all will be well.

By something of a contrast, the Cups Two can bring us a quite different energy and set of circumstances. Here we see a clear image of what we have previously described as 'complementary opposites', in the man and woman who often feature on this card gazing deeply into each other's eyes! They are usually sharing a cup of love or friendship and demonstrating the mutual equality and love between them. Their twin poles of energy are equal and opposite and it is in this that balance and wholeness is found.

This wholeness is something we must each find ourselves, looking within to balance the outer and although the energy of this card can manifest in a relationship or at least this level of understanding with someone, this can only succeed if each are equally whole within themselves first.

This in turn requires that any arguments or discord we have experienced in our lives be dealt with, settled and released from ourselves especially but any we interact with as well. Mutual benefit and trust should replace the above scenarios as we open to absorb the pleasant quality of energy that this card brings. From here we learnt to see, value and appreciate the value of others in our lives, what they bring to us and us to them.

Co-operation is a key ingredient of this energy and again this needs to apply with ourselves and with others. It is a good time to consider if we are in conflict with ourselves in any way, especially emotionally and what we might need to do to resolve this. This brings us to this state of self-love and emotional affinity with others as we learn to abide by the contracts we make with ourselves at this time.

The energy of this card also has the ability to cross barriers and divisions between people, at a racial and social level as well as in friendships, relationships and families. This balancing energy must be maintained carefully and we should avoid any sense of possessiveness or dependency that seeks to strangle and kill that loving sense we have established now.

We can liken this energy here to being a little like the emergence of spring after a winter. Harshness and cold thaws and a warmer sense is opened to and welcomed. There are signs of hope and openness is again possible. This card has been likened to a lesser version of the Lovers in the Major Arcana but its effect and influence should be taken as a lesser thing, but perhaps more simple and pure in its essence.

With the Swords Two it is more of a meeting of minds than hearts that comes to the fore with this card and that is required. Perhaps as a result of the way in which we can respond to mental energies, the influence of this card is seen as more of a limiting than uniting one. Due to the nature of the energy of two, this card can bring with it a limit to our thoughts with unclear decisions and an indecisive mind.

However a defensive approach and attitude can swiftly and easily be turned into attack and a positive response.

The energy of this card can bring about deadlocked thoughts but change is of course inevitable. The trick is to make the change of our own choosing. It is good to weigh up the potential outcomes we can create for ourselves here, before acting. This allows us to use the energy of two to our advantage. There can be times when we have to rely on our intuition rather than logic here, this being a blend of logic and feeling, head and heart. From this process we can see that from inertia and defence come truth and the creation of our own reality.

We should also be careful at this time not to enter into an agreement that does not resonate with us and here again our inner-tuition can be called upon to guide us. We should look within and question our motives to ensure these are based on our own truth, whatever this may be at the time. If there is any deceit then we can be sure this comes from us and will affect us more than anyone else.

The two swords featured in this card can be seen as the two opposing forces that keep conflict at bay, truth again being the watchword for our response. The concentration required to do this can be called upon here and then released so the energy around our situation can flow, to bring about the desired change and result. The positive values we do hold within us can be deployed to create that outcome.

A soft and gentle breeze may be blowing through our lives with this card but it not destructive, merely fanning the flames of required change. To resist creates an unnecessary conflict and if we need to alter our direction to go with the air, it will be so much the easier path for us. There may be a need for some release as we do this but we will surely find this is necessary and ultimately to our advantage. New possibilities can be seen swiftly, even if the full outcome may still be some way off. With due care and diligence we can move on and this card can bring a significant step forward.

With the Rods Two we can see a chance to develop our personalities and form an idea from the Ace into something workable. The spark from the fire has been fanned to a flame and it now seeks fuel, direction and purpose. Fire can of course be a purifying force or one of destruction. Our mind has given us a workable idea and our task here is to use the energy to further develop and even begin to act on what we know.

This can be seen as a time of making necessary preparations for success so this card brings with it a positive energy. Here we can weigh up the possibilities and see what sits right within us. We need to ensure we do not allow things and the energy to stagnate around what we are experiencing or we may become stuck. We need to be careful that we do not lose energy or enthusiasm so that the flame that has been nurtured does not go out. A loss of faith in the self at this stage can result in a lost opportunity.

Equally, once some progress is made and the energy of the two responded to in a positive, enhancing way, we can gain strength of will and confidence. This helps us to become a little more self-aware and a little more complete. We begin to believe that we can take an idea and turn it into reality. There can be a need because of this to have some degree of self-control and to take responsibility for ourselves in a way that may not have been done before, regardless of any expectation of outcome.

There may need to be consideration of joining forces with others or accepting help that can be offered, which is all for the positive. If we see this card as showing us that desire plus thought equals truth we can go a long way to its successful outcome. Now is a time when the 'courage of our convictions' can be demonstrated and some self-awareness and knowledge can be gained.

Equally we should ensure that we do not fall into the early trappings of the ego here and allow a lust for power and control to dictate our actions. Rather we need to focus on negotiation and compromise, two strong facets of this energy. Equal exchange is always a positive outcome so everyone gains and this card illustrates this well. Should this not be the case then the goals held at this time can soon be seen as empty and false ones.

The result of this energy can be a galvanising force to move forward, out of any inertia, which can manifest as an increased zest for life and drive within. With a clear decision based on supportive and positive values, the client can use the energy of two to set themselves up to move forwards to the best possible outcome.

THREES

 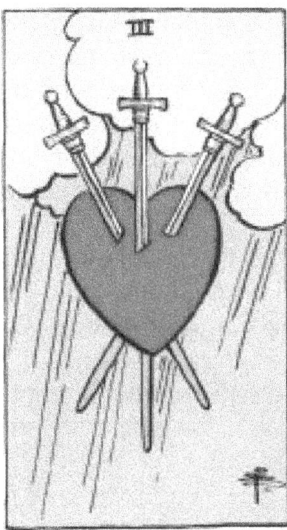

Many people say that things happen in Three's and as we are about to see this is indeed, very true. We will see that this has been the case throughout history and with good reason.

When we look first at the influence of the number itself, we can see that three can be seen as a welcome and positive influence, since it can repair the damage done by the division that two brought. This overcoming of the duality leads to a new integration, just as in the way that male and female invariably results in child! Perhaps this is why Three is often regarded as 'heaven's dearest number'.

Three is the first number to produce a geometric shape when displayed diagrammatically. This is of course, the triangle and correctly an equilateral one. The triangle is enclosed by three points and formed from three lines. If we now explore that trinity a little further we can see the extent to which we have always seen things in three's and the way the Universe is naturally geared to this way of operating.

Firstly, many in the Christian world see the Divinity in three aspects, such as Father, Son and Holy Spirit but this is also true in many other religions and mythological traditions too. If we go back to paganism, from a time before Christianity existed, the Goddess, as the Mother of All, was seen as having three aspects, Maiden, Mother and Crone. The god of magic and inventor of writing was known as 'Hermes Trimegistos' or 'Thrice Great Hermes'. The Buddhist tradition has three sources of salvation, being Buddha, Dharma and Samgha. The Sufi way of mortals was to follow three paths: Divine law, the mystical path and reality.

The Bible exemplifies this threefold way of natural phenomena repeatedly. Jonah spent three days in the whale, Egypt was subjected to three days in darkness, Paul was in ecstasy for three days after his conversion, there were three magicians who travelled to Jesus' birth, Jesus himself being know as 'the way, the truth and the life' and indeed he appeared to his disciples three times after his death, Peter denying him three times, then rising to heaven after three days. Animal sacrifices, Biblical, Greek or Roman were practised in threes.

The same is true in the Holy Grail legends. In the Temple of the Grail there are three gates, those of faith, chastity and humility and three Knights eventually find the Grail. In the shamanic traditions across the world, although they go by different names, there are essentially three worlds, the Underworld, Middleworld and Upperworld. The Moon is seen as having three phases; Waxing, Full and Waning.

Many ancient and scared texts also illustrate our threefold principle here. The Indian Upanishads have three aspects of the Divine, being, thinking and bliss, with three human faculties, hearing, understanding and knowledge. Lao Tzu told us that the 'Tao produces unity, unity produces duality, duality produces trinity and this triad produces all things'. The Zohar tells us that the world was created from wisdom, reason and perception.

Life itself is seen as having a beginning, middle and end and time has past, present and future. In philosophy and psychology three is the number for classification, being done by time, space and causality. In chemistry there are three classifications of matter, acids, bases and salts whilst physics uses mass, power and velocity. Science generally recognises three states, solid, liquid and gaseous and three principles of active, middle and passive. To plot a point anywhere we need length, height and width.

In creation all things can be classed as mineral, plant or animal. A fruit has husk, flesh and kernel whilst plants have root, shaft and flower. In our language we have noun, verb and adjective as well as thought, word and deed. Our folk tales tell us of the three wise monkeys and our children know of Goldilocks and the three bears and the three blind mice. We eat three meals a day, wait for three lights at traffic lights, 3 strikes when we are out, win gold, silver or bronze medals before three orders to start a race! We might receive three cheers having put 'blood, sweat and tears' into it. We might then say it has been as easy as 'one, two, three' or that it was our 'third time lucky'.

So we see all too easily how the energy of three works its way through all things and all aspects of our lives, society and beliefs. When we work with the energy of three at its different levels then we have some powerful forces at our disposal. We may need to confront any blockages we have before us and learn to express ourselves truly. Three gives us the chance for the fullest of self-expression and now we can see how we may do this through the cards.

The image on the traditional showing of Pentacles Three is one of refuge and retreat, being set within a church. However the active energy here is to spur the client on to achievement and material building. This inner drive to progress and success in the material world can bring a certain satisfaction within although this can be coupled with a desire for more and new experiences. With sincere and focussed effort great things can be aimed for now. This is a time to break free of any previously held restraints and place their mark on the world.

Although this may still be a time of apprenticeship or learning, perfection can be aimed for. The energy of this card can create good and positive opportunities for business ventures and commercial enterprises of all kinds. The ground for future prosperity can be laid now, the key factor being the craft, skill and ability of the individual. We may find that help comes now from others as the combined effort creates a bigger goal. Positive help and cooperation can be used and here we have an opportunity for finding our true vocation and maximising talent and ability. Attention to detail may also be required as the energy here allows us to step out into the big wide world with all that we have to offer. With a combination of practical work and spiritual integrity this energy is allowed its fullest expression. So this card can be seen as showing us the fruits of our labour.

The appearance of this card usually brings a smile as indeed the image is of a cheery nature, prompting us to say 'Cheers' as we see the cups raised. The overall feel here is one of creativity, abundance, pleasure and beauty.

This energy usually brings a cause for celebration and a rich bounty of positive emotion. So it is that the Cups Three can be seen as a precursor to marriage, relationships and birth. The energy is certainly a fertile one and this energy should be utilised to the highest degree. There is a strong healing force now and a mood of trust and harmony and any separations can be reconciled now, whether with ourselves or others.

Hedonism and the pleasures of the senses can overtake us now so there is a need for some restraint and common sense as we allow ourselves to respond to this rising tide of good feeling. There may be a need to guard a little against being carried away with the love of the moment, in whatever way. Along with exploiting one's own feelings it is also vital to ensure we do not exploit others at an emotional level, as this can be a temptation with the energy here.

The energy here is also strongly pulled towards family and friends. Reunions, celebrations and so forth are all indicated as they are an expression of the generosity of spirit that can arise now. There can be a certain magnetism about people when they experience the energy of this card that pulls others towards them. This can be a productive experience for all, but care should also be taken to ensure others do not just take.

This can also be the energy of the empath, which can be a surprisingly difficult one to deal with. Others feelings can be all too easily felt and absorbed into the self, and if this remains unchecked it can all too easily become overwhelming. Once this is responded to in a healthy way, using energetic and practical protection and strengthening techniques, the higher experience of unselfish, unconditional love can be experienced.

The overall experience of this card is one of peace and plenty, at an emotional level, offering as it does the source of sustenance that each needs and requires. Emotions can be heightened, in whatever way and once we learn to respond positively to these we can emerge fresh and revitalised for the task that lies ahead.

As we work our way energetically now to the level of mind, with the strong emotional emphasis we have just experienced, it is easy to see how the energy of this card can result in a conflict between head and heart. Indeed the typical and alarming image of this card, with the three swords piercing a blood red heart, can be an apt demonstration of this.

Often we find when we work with the energy of this card, our head pulls us in one direction and our heart the other. As we saw with the energy of the number three, it is in the combination or result of the two opposing poles that we find our resolution. The blend of thought and feeling give us a more intuitive approach, our own inner truth which will always guide us if we pause to listen.

Often what is required is to step aside from emotions, which can be aggressive or twisted now and from total logic which can be cold and calculating and focus instead to that which lies beneath both of these. This is where the productive solution that is inherent in the energy of this card can be found. It has the gift of directing us towards that which we know to be true within us.

Another need that can arise is that of outward bound communication, there having been something of an implosion in this area likely with this card. The Swords are directed inwards and this shows us that there can be a tendency towards isolation, both emotionally and mentally. Possessive feelings, hurt, jealousy, anger and the like should all be guarded against being allowed to take control over the head and heart now.

The message of this card is rather like the fresh breeze that whilst it may stir things up just a little and not be readily welcomed, is a necessary force to dislodge what may have become stuck and scatter these energies enough so they need to be dealt with.

With Rods we enter a more positive approach than the conflict indicated and experienced through Swords. With the surge of heat and passion that fire brings we now feel that flowing through our veins, causing us to look ahead and envision our future. Intention can be all important now as what we focus on creating through the energy we expend will shape the reality that we create for our future. So this card is very much a case of 'as we sow so shall we reap'.

The more deeply we can dig now, the more we reap the rewards. The energy of this card offers us a great deal by way of potential and fuel for our fire. If we can utilise this to our best effect we can create plans far beyond what we may have previously thought possible. This is an excellent time to learn the truth that we create our own reality and indeed to create a reality that is wonderful.

It is important not to become trapped in the stage of planning and not taking action so that we do not miss out on the reality and establishment that we are about to see with the Four. Three is a creative energy that causes us to do things and it is important that we respond to this. This may be creative and will require us to draw on our inner resources but the energy of this card fully supports us in this process.

FOURS

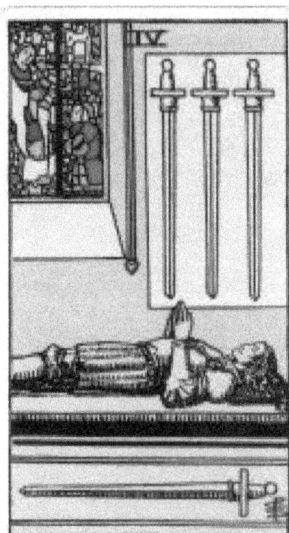

The energy here can cause us to feel full of life and full of vigour and enthusiasm, so it is important now that we consider what we are focussed upon and how we are using that fire within. When used for a common and higher good we automatically pull towards us energies and forces that further fuel our fire

This energy, seen as that of the creator or inventor helps us turns our dreams into reality, so now we need to see what we are dreaming of and if that is truly the reality we wish to create. With a controlled intention and intent we can find ourselves somehow in the right place at the right time. The question now is how will we respond to this?

Here we enter the realm of the material, established world, the number for logic, reason and all things measurable. As we will see, so many things work in multiples of four in our world and are indeed divided the same way. It is clear that since ancient times the particular energy that four brings is central to the structure and working of the everyday world of which we are a part.

It is easy to see this when we consider the four (main) directions about us and the four winds that blow from them throughout our four seasons. There are four primary colours linked to these directions too. Modern science recognises four states of matter, being solid, liquid, gases and plasma and the human being itself is seen as having four levels within us, those of physical, emotional, mental and spiritual.

Pythagoras saw four as the ideal number since if you add all of its components, you are given unity i.e. $1 + 2 + 3 + 4 = 10$. Geometrically, four is expressed as a square and the structure of four gives us the first time we can see spatial dimensions, shape no longer being flat; from length, breadth, depth and height.

The earliest humans were known to have identified four phases of the Moon, being crescent, waxing, full and waning, and to have organised their time phases around this. If we look at ancient people's structure we know that Mayan settlements were organised with four roads leading out from a sacred tree at the centre, in these four directions, with four shrines at the exit points. Many traditions across the world speak of their being four ages of history.

The Celtic 'equal-armed cross' has its four arms and this glyph was the Egyptian symbol for immortality in its hieroglyphic language, being a symbol for the spiritual in the cosmos. The Etruscans used the same symbol for global power.

The Egyptian god Amun-Ra was known as the Lord of the Four Directions. The Indian god Shiva has four arms and in the Hindu tradition there are four castes of society, and four rivers of paradise, as well as four streams of milk that flow from the four udders of the sacred cow. The Muslims see the human being as having four natural qualities as well as elements, seasons, humours, directions, winds and minerals, much like our Western view.

In Islam there are four scared books whilst the Sufi have four steps on their ascent to the Divine. In the Qaballah there are also four worlds, whilst the Zuni and Sioux Native American nations have a fourfold division of human life too, along with four classes of animal life.

Biblically, we see much of the energy of four too. Ezekiel's vision was of four creatures, the man, lion, bull and eagle, which we have seen transferred as elemental symbols on The World card. Noah saw rain for 40 day and nights, along with the Four Horsemen of the Apocalypse as told in the last of the four gospels.

In our modern language we need a good, square meal every day and can be required to square up to those who oppose us. This may take us back to square one and we need to square our accounts so we can stand four square and solid, squarely on the ground.

So it is we can see that when we work with the energy of four we are dealing with issues of security which are achieved by a steady and patient effort through a gradual, consolidatory process working towards our goals. Four helps us build a solid and stable foundation, find our security and establish commitment and clarity to what we're doing. It is a very grounding energy and without this we are likely to crumble and fail at the first opposition we encounter. Once established with careful steps and precision, we can build high but for now the need is to focus on what lies immediately before us. Four brings strength, vigour and vitality as these we need now. This energy shows us our boundaries and gives us security.

As we look at how this is expressed through each card we can see that the foundation in the Pentacles Four can be literal ones. This suit being of a practical nature we see that the four here is expressed through physical, practical security, through mediums such as work and house and home. This card can be rather like the experience of kicking off one's shoes at the end of a day stood and relaxing with your favourite drink.

The inner security needed with the four takes place on the outside, at least initially with this card. This established life with its regularity and structure provides the foundation for the individual to move on from there. So here 'home is where the heart is', as is the bank balance with the energy here. Being of the suit of Coins, it is easy for us at this stage to become too dependent or obsessive of money and use this as a crux for the deeper security that is required. It may be that some energy is required to be given to financial matters but not to excess.

Traditionally the card of the miser, here we can see that this is more about a need for security on that inner level, the outer behaviour being a mask of fear from facing this need. Once established of course the security acts as the antidote to that fear and we can move forward. This can then make this a good time for business and financial dealings, with investments likely to pay off.

Fear of material and practical security can be a more common thing these days as we experience what seems to this author to be an all too obvious collapse of capitalism. The bigger picture, of which at best we seem to know little, would seem to my mind to suggest however that this is a good thing as we will need to learn to base ourselves and practical lives on the common good as well as individual gain. Perhaps it is then that we will see more of this card, especially since at the time of writing this we are entering the fabled year of 2012.

When we are secure within ourselves we can follow that maxim we have seen before of 'as within, so without' and the outer will flow more naturally and work with us, rather than us trying to base our lives and living on fear, insecurity and/or greed. The Pentacles Four then, has much to teach us.

As do all Tarot cards of course, and the Cups Four is therefore no exception. One of the principle things we can learn here is that if we base our emotional well-being on fear or on seeing only the negative, then that is what we are far more likely to experience. It is all too easy, especially in these apparently negative and threatening times, to see what we do not have rather than what we do, so the message that this card can bring us is to do just that: look at what is positive, what we do know and love about ourselves, rather than on the gaps we might feel that exist in our personality and selves.

There can be a strong energy of boredom here and an apathy that can result from the sense of resignation that the energy of this card can bring. This sense of 'oh what's the point' can cloud our perception of reality and we can assume things that are not true, usually about ourselves. The simple joy of being alive can be threatened now and we may need to dig deep to find this again. Be mindful now that this spark can never be put out, however it may be dimmed.

Once we find a sense of compassion and love for ourselves, which is one of the chief messages of this card, we also gain an ability to empathise with others. This can make us a more complete, understanding and basically loving person, rooted in the strength of self-knowledge, awareness and above all, love. A lack of self-love, or perhaps more accurately, a perception of self-loathing can be an all too common causal factor for much errant behaviour we see around us now The security and sense of security within that comes from self-love acts as such a powerful antidote to all this and is really one of the basic lessons on the spiritual path, no matter who we are or what we have done or believe about ourselves, Once we find this for the self, we find it for others and the world is instantly a better place.

Just as our emotional view of ourselves will have a huge bearing on how we feel on a day to day basis, so it is true of our state of mind too, as illustrated with the Swords Four. Many people take a critical view of themselves when asked what they think about who they are. The mind seems to have a natural tendency to always be active and to always be critical and negative. If there are faults to find or objections to raise, you can always look to the human mind to find them!

One of the best remedies for this is to look towards quietening the mind and slowing down the flow of those troubled and disruptive thoughts. The energy of this card brings a need for stillness of thought, control of the mind and a sense of security at this level. It is widely accepted amongst many spiritual traditions that there is a link between the breath and the mind, so here we can look to learning breathing techniques to aid us in our quest now. Once we have become familiar with these we can then add to our arsenal with the practice of meditation.

Many people baulk at the idea of this and of the whole concept of 'emptying one's mind (I've never been sure mine had much in it to empty!). However if we accept the basic idea that we will not empty the mind or clear it as if often said to be required for meditation and instead just let ourselves relax, breathe fully and deeply for a bit, close our eyes and just let ourselves rest, we find a much easier gateway to meditation, free of fluffy concepts and ideals.

Over a period of time (it takes three weeks to form a habit) we can learn to make more of a friend of our mind. This will allow us to find a sense of security there and a place of peace and tuition when needed. This strength of mind can serve us to an amazing degree, quite apart from the benefits a regular meditation or relaxation practice brings us. The need to shelter or cocoon ourselves away reduces and instead we can be free and open in our minds, letting the light into what may have been a dark place.

So the process of getting to know ourselves continues as we open ourselves to the energy of the Rods Four. Here it is as if we are asked the question 'who and what are you' by the Universe. The security issues raised by the energy of four have caused us to come to know more of who we are by looking at what we are doing with the Pentacles, how we are feeing with Cups, what we are thinking with Swords and now what the result of all this is, with Rods.

Fire being the energy it is, will provoke and push us to be ourselves and we are pushed now to see where and how our overall sense of self originates from. In other words, what makes us the person we are and are we OK with this? The energy here promises us much in the sense of teaching us these things, if we care too look a little more deeply within.

The basic tenet of the card here is that we need to look within, not without to find our sense of self, our security and place in the world. In essence we could just simply say 'what fuels our fire' and see how we respond, or perhaps how do we give fuel to our own fire. Once lit, we need to ensure our own particular and individual fire does not go, especially in the darkest moments and this card challenges us now to see how we will continue to ensure a plentiful supply of fuel. If you are unsure, look again, for we are all born with the inner fuel we need, it is only us that can lose, or misplace it.

FIVES

As we move into Five we enter an altogether more positive and affirming energy since Five is seen as the number of life itself and of love and the soul. Five is seen as the number for natural humanity, perhaps linked here with our five senses. Significantly it is the first number to be made of an odd and even number in combination, from the masculine 2 and the feminine 3, it therefore representing the union of male and female. This may be why Jung saw this number as representing natural humanity.

Five shows itself all around us in nature in many ways too. We can see it in flower petals, commonly in groups of five as well of course as our own fingers and toes. We are reminded of starfish too and cauliflower and broccoli are clumped in fives. If you cut crossways through an apple or pear you can see the shape of five presented magically.

The geographical representation of Five is of course the five-pointed star, or pentagram. Used as a symbol of protection for thousands of years and thought to be Egyptian in origin, the pentagram is widely seen now in many guises. Paracelsus used it and when drawn as a single line it represents endless love.

In mythology Five was linked to the Goddess Ishtar, whose Roman equivalent was Venus, Equally many traditions had close links to Five. The Mayan settlements were laid out in four directions, the fifth point being found at its sacred centre. In India there were five points to the cross, inclusive of the centre, which offered protection against evil. There were materials for worship, five destructive implements, elders in a village and five collections of fables with their five teachings.

The Sikhs had five sacred objects and there were five books of Moses. Persian poetry featured epics in groups of five. Aristotle himself postulated five virtues to human nature and the Islamic faith preached prayer five times a day, offered five pillars of faith, five categories of law, five prophets and archangels and even dictated that the booty of war was split five ways!

Chinese life was also based on the energy of five. There were five sacred mountains, five kinds of grain, degrees of nobility, virtues, kinds of fortune, moral qualities, classical books, weapons and punishments. So it is easy to see how five is the number for life.

As we know we have our own fourfold nature, being physical, emotional, mental and spiritual. But if we blend these together we reach their quintessence, meaning the 'fifth-being, known as the 'flag of life'. This is what the Greeks called the Five Pentad.

In our modern society we visit five-star hotels, see five-star plays and eat in five-star restaurants, or at least some do; the rest of us wish we did! Many people aspire to 'stardom' and when excelling can give stellar performances, making them a new star on the horizon. It is important they do not become star struck in their rise to being a rock star or sports star. Once a superstar however, they have made it! The US Army gives us five star generals and we see this powerful image on many flags and corporate logos across the world.

When we experience and work with the energy of Five there can be a challenge to be who we truly are, which we learn through lessons of freedom and discipline. It is through inner discipline that we find our sense of self and freedom from that which limits us. We require focus and a depth of experience. We are challenged through our dependence to find independence! There is a need to avoid routine which can feel like imprisonment and equally to avoid over indulgence. Our experience teaches us the focus and discipline we need as we acquire the wide range of skills to equip us for life. Five was seen as a rebellious number since early times and so it is that through its energy we can temper ourselves as we experience who we are.

This rebellion we speak of can be seen as a reaction to the limits imposed in the Four so we can welcome this interruption, intrusion and change that Five brings. It may be seen as an interference but it a necessary one, lest we remain forever in boring four! It may bring instability but this is temporary and it also brings a vital catalyst. Removal of restriction and security can be painful, rather like tearing a plaster off our skin, but the sting soon fades and we see healing as a result. So it is that as we examine the energy of each card we can see how we face our obstacles in their various and welcome ways.

In the Pentacles Five we see a need for healing as the result of the impact of the energy on a physical level. This somewhat negative response presupposes that the individual has allowed his fixed rigidity with the four to affect him to such an extent that something has manifested physically, hence the need for healing. This is the power of the Five, which comes in to shake things up at the everyday level.

Other ways in which this might manifest is a need to change one's diet, give up smoking, alcohol etc, change job or career, move home and so on. The point to grasp here is that on the material level things have been allowed to rest and remain secure for perhaps too long and too much. Hence the need for the energy of five to invade and strip this security in its particular pot down to the basics once more. It is then for the individual to step up to the plate and respond as best they may.

Of course if things are still left, since we know that the nature of energy is to flow and so it will do, coming out in some physical form that speaks plainly of where the person is resisting the change of five. Once this is identified and understood appropriate response can be made and healing will occur.

Boredom can be a big factor with the energy preceding this card. It is very easy to lose motivation and that spark of being really alive that keeps us evolving and embracing change. Thankfully the energy of five prevents us from wallowing in this too long if we do find ourselves in this particular sand pit or mire. There can be a need to break free of restriction and break down barriers, step out of the norm and into the unfamiliar. Do not rest on your laurels now, for they have rested too long. See past the discomfort of change and embrace the new. The earth may shake beneath you but if you learn to flow with it, you'll be fine.

Emotionally this energy can also stir us up somewhat. There can be a strong energy of emotional boredom as well as physical and perhaps some fear of stepping out of one's comfort zone. There can be a distinct lack of interest in what is happening around the client which shows a need for reassessment. With the pushiness that five brings, if we do not respond then we are provoked until we do. Emotional upheaval can be unpleasant and disturbing but the message and energy of this card is clear in that it tells us we cannot remain stuck as we are forever as this saps the very life force out of us and the Universe is not structured to remain as it is. As part of that great living force, that includes us.

We are in the realm of water here of course and I am reminded of the river that will simply not be held in the film 'Out of Africa', the greater wisdom eventually realised that the river in question simply does not want to go that way! This card brings much the same energy to us. You may have found a place of security that feels comforting and safe but this does not mean it can stay that way forever. Five trundles in here to ensure this is the case.

There is a big question here as to how we see our experiences, basically either as loss, wring our hands and crying 'woe is me' to the heavens or we can shrug our shoulders, give a wry smile and think 'oh well, that's that then'! With the former we are simply likely to experience more loss until we learn to let go within. With the latter we can see new chances and opportunities opening up and indeed, learn to take our chances.

Of course this may signal the end of at least a phase in your relationship, if not the thing itself. This may not be a sad or bad thing of course, it may simply have run its course and there is a need on both sides to open up to someone new. So rather than having two unfulfilled people we can instead create four happy ones!

So rather than seeing the negative and seeing all as an 'attraction of tragedy' we can instead see the sun rising, to a new dawn, a new day, of unknown hope, possibility and adventure. There is a similar message with Swords Five too, albeit of course at a mental level. We can make a choice as to whether we see things as a defeat or success.

Mental control and strength of mind are important things we can gain from the experience of the energy here. It may be that the energy of five causes us to think or feel that we lack control or are out of control of our minds and our thinking, Sometimes it is by letting go and admitting to ourselves that we just don't have the answers or know what is what and which way is up anymore, that we can create a blank canvas in our minds on which to project and then experience our new reality.

We can indeed be our own worst enemies, even though the traditional image of this card warns against treachery. From the therapeutic viewpoint however, we tend to internalise this and see ourselves as needing to take responsibility for our own minds and state of mental health. If we find others seem to be on the attack then, this is usually because we have a need to learn and see another's standpoint or at the very least broaden our thinking and open our minds.

It may be that we need to release old ways of thinking and perhaps even experience some grief and admit that we did not have all the answers or even, god forbid, that we were wrong! With just a little humility, something that can be sadly lacking in today's ego-driven world of instant everything, we can win great victories.

So one of the ways we can respond to this card is to take the stance of 'weathering the storm' that seems to be ruffling our mental feathers at this time. However it may be that what we can really learn from the experience of this energy is that, no matter how we feel or what our thoughts are, we do always have a choice of how to see things and how to respond. The energy of this card can teach us this powerful and mentally liberating truth.

So it is with the Rods Five that the question of how we then use this new found power that Swords has given us arises. It certainly seems to be the case when we look at history that 'power corrupts' and we would do well to be mindful of this as we draw in the energy of this card and it appears in our reading.

The Five here does its best to stir us up so that we can see who we are and learn to wield the strength of that to our best advantage. The maxim that 'out of chaos comes order' can apply here as we learn to give a new structure to the apparent chaos, internal or external, that the energy of Rods Five brings. As we learn to harness these seemingly disparate forces so it is we can construct a new focus and power that propels us forward to what awaits.

We may need to use our faculties of cunning and guile now. We may need to turn to our intuition and follow these inner promptings as the energy here reaches and prompts us. This will ensure we do not fall foul of any corruption or ego based impulses. By doing so we can find that we rise above competition, aggression and opposition which may all rear their respectively ugly heads now and so it is that the smoother progress of the Six comes into view, as we stand, a little bruised and battered, blinking at the light of that new dawn.

SIXES

When we come to Six we are confronted with what is regarded as the perfect number for the created world. This is because it is the sum and product of its parts, in the view of the mathematicians, being the product of the first male number, two and the first female number, three.

The Bible contains many references that can help us understand this energy. In the beginning of course, God created the world in six days. In the Old Testament, Isiah's vision was of the seraphim with six wings. Jesus' crucifixion took six days and six hours, which we are told elsewhere later developed into the siesta from the root 'sexta' meaning 'rest in the afternoon'. Matthew tells us that six is the symbol of the 'vita activa' - the life of good works. In the book of Revelations we have six angels blowing their trumpets to herald the Last Judgement. There are also of course twelve disciples, the mathematics of which I do not think need justification!

The symbol of the six pointed star is an ancient representation of the energy of six. Also known as the Star of David, this consists of one upward and one downward pointing arrow, being male and female respectively. This symbolises the union of creation and destruction.

In Native American society, the tepee represented the calendar, being formed around 12 poles, as did the tepee, and we also have our 12 zodiac signs of course. The Native Americans also consisted of 12 nation tribes, each with 12 clans per tribe.

In the world around us we see six represented in many ways. The shape of the hexagon is found in nature in beehives, showing its relationship to structure and order. We have learned to replicate this in the shape of nuts and bolts, woven baskets, umbrellas, caps and even parachutes! We can also see the hexagon if we slice the top of tomatoes, carrots and peppers and also in the virus under a microscope. The shape of the honeycomb is also seen in aspirin, vitamin c and snowflakes, at a chemical level. Insects also have six legs.

Our old currency had 12 shillings to a pound and 12 pence to a shilling. Multiples of six are also strewn across our timing methods, with 60 seconds to a minute and 60 of these to an hour of course. We also have 12 chemical steps in every spiral turn of the DNA helix. The Chinese also work to 12 meridian energy channels in the body and there are 12 cranial nerves in the head. All this shows us how central the energy of six is in it various forms, to the nature of structure and order.

The nature of six thus lends itself to looking at out life structure and our ideals and visions when we work with this energy. This energy pushes us to accept our practical reality and do what is needed to bring this into line with our vision. More personally it is about accepting our self and our world as it is and doing what we then can with it. We learn to see the bigger picture and observe our priorities in line with this. This is the number for dreamers and writers, to give hope and direction. There is a need to avoid extremes now and to avoid judgement, of the self and others. If we learn to lighten up and become flexible we can indeed fulfil those dreams and visions.

Six can be seen as the time when we turn the enemies we made with Five into friends. In this way we join forces rather than divide them and form a new idealism and strive for perfection. We search for and find common ground, using the energy and concept of synergy. We begin to experience some sense of satisfaction at whatever level the six energy operates within us (which suit appears in the reading).

Let's see how this is played out at each level. We begin as always with the realm of Earth, the Pentacles. This physical level is where we can experience some pleasure with the six, whether on a purely physical level or more materially. As we know the Pentacles energy is to do with tangibility so here the positive, forward-moving energy of the six can bring some material gain, This is not to any sense of excess or luxury at this stage, but the Universe here seems to be about educating us to realise the principle of 'equal profit and loss'. Part of this seems to be that in order to realise this gain we first need to be not holding on to our finance and even giving some of it away!

In these times of materiality, greed, bonuses, million pound wage structures and higher property prices, the idea of actually giving some of your hard-earned loot away can seem to go against the grain. However this is not the grain that the Universe runs by. The flow of the Universe is actually just that, a flow and by allowing the physical manifestation of this flow, at this time in the form of money, to indeed, flow through us, we can find the fulfilment of this energy here. Of course it is one of those oxymorons that means that the more of this flow we can open to, the more filthy lucre seems to flow to us!

This card can indicate a time when the client can experience many demands on their time and energy and as with that flow above, the need here is to let go of struggle and get into the flow again. If they are able to do this then the Universe duly provides the necessary energy and harmony. This is the energy of six and once we click with it, it can indeed be a joyful experience. When we are in the flow of the Universe after all, there cannot be much better.

It is time when the energy of this card comes into your life to bring the spirit of Scrooge, being taunted by any spirits of miserliness, in past, present of future! Enjoy the success that comes your way and revel in the flow of good fortune you may find now. Harvest what you can and be ready to give freely and happily to those more needy and less blessed than you.

With the Cups Six we find that we have entered an altogether friendlier realm of the sharing, caring kind. This card brings a rather childlike quality that can be quite a delight to experience, It is a time of innocence, purity and hope, the combination of these qualities creating the expression of the energy we find at this point.

When we feel the energy of this card in ourselves and life we can find that, although it may be a fragile one, there is a sense of well-being within. If we can dig a little deeper we find that this quality can be held and strengthened. It may be that the only way we can find expression of this is in a childlike innocence but there is a beauty and purity in this quality that hurdles explanation.

We can also find that, almost magically, we draw those to us who are the equal of ourselves. This exchange of energies is actually an expression of the nature of the Universe. Just as with money, the more we try to hold on to good feelings and keep them within, the less we experience them. Instead, if we can allow ourselves to surrender to the feeling (or the pounds!) we find that the flow this creates allows the Universe to 'do its thing' and a natural flow ensues.

With the progressive energy that comes with the Six, our feelings are not bound to stay this way forever. As we learn to express how we are feeling and show who we truly are, so our feelings develop and progress. Put a different way, the more love we give, the more we experience. So it is we can find that the people we draw to ourselves and into our lives at this time share that identity and understanding, even if they do not know why.

It is important to recognise that the stage we have arrived at is partly due to the past or previous experiences we have learned from and assimilated. We can realise some of our emotional dreams now and this only serves to garner the good feelings and bounty we have. The past creates the future and with the energy of this card we are caught at the moment the two coincide. Emotional pleasure is the result we have,

Outwardly we can then see that this may be experienced by way of renewed friendships, new acquaintances and connections with others. This is a meeting of hearts rather than minds which is where we shift ourselves to the attention of the Swords. I have heard so many Tarot readers over the years say that 'you are heading to calmer or smoother waters. Every time I hear this regurgitated, I know the Swords Six has appeared!

The card shows a ferryman rowing a couple across imminently choppy waters but they are heading where all is calm and clear. We know now that the water shows our emotions, which may indeed have been turbulent but due to some effort of will and mental application we have sought understanding and resolution in the mind, this being the realm and level of this card. Perhaps then a better statement to offer is that of asking the client what they have been missing, what have they not been 'getting' or understanding and what do they need to make more effort with to see a different point of view.

This is at once empowering and supportive, rather than a blanket term that offers them a hope based on no fact. Now they have something to go away and work with and this essentially is the different between what I grandly call Tarot Therapy and fortune-telling. However, climbing back off my soap box once more, we can see that communication can be a key factor with this card.

92

There is a need sometimes to re-open negotiation that may have ceased or to enter into some form of communication with a different attitude and approach to before. This will be one reconciliation and of seeking progress. This perhaps must first occur in the heart, given the propensity of water on the card but follow through to the mind, which needs then to be open to receive as well as heard. If this is not present, but only a desire to work things out, this makes an effective opening statement in itself and the rest can then follow.

Obstacles that may appear can be overcome and again we can experience that magical quality inherent in the Universe as we saw with the Cups Six, whereby the right words or thought can come to us at just the right time to help us understand. This understanding can result in the peace of mind spoken of earlier and we can breathe fully, perhaps for the first time in a long time, and relax.

We may also be the recipient of some timely and good advice when under the influence of this card and we can again ask the client what they are not hearing. A closed mind does not often hear the truth and the energy of this card begets and demands the truth. We can learn with the energy we are experiencing now the power of objectivity and create a bridge over that troubled water so beloved of readers everywhere!

As we learn the mental lessons of our past so we can turn to a future with understanding, openness and willingness to grow and learn. Our horizons can be opened up to beautiful new vistas and clarity is ours for the taking, The trick then is to consider positively what we will do with that new found wisdom?

This can be positively played if we have learned to absorb the energy of the Rods Six, this being the higher level the Minor Arcana reaches. This card is usually trumpeted as 'success after a battle', given its depiction of a victory parade supposedly following the said battle. However as we tend to turn inwards with the therapeutic approach we can see that the intended victory needs to occur within ourselves.

The more we fight our demons, the more struggle we get, or put another way, what we resist, persists. This does not mean that we should give in to our demons and just indulge ourselves with whatever our chosen vice may be. Rather we find that we can have the victory we speak of here if we simply accept that part of our character, love it anyway and we then find that its control over us diminishes. We find that our demon is not so terrible after all and we can learn to befriend it, or them. Once we do this, we start to see that rather than being motivated by fear, we are motivated by love; primarily love of ourselves.

As there is a direct reflection between what we experience on the inside, this inner love is experienced on the outside with a greater openness, softness and love being shared with those we encounter. The Six energy is one in which it is fair to say that there is a turnaround from the past to the future and here we can learn to fuel our fire in a different direction. Rather than focussing our anger and fear we can shift to an energy of love and serenity within,

To start this process we can ask ourselves what we are fearful of and what we may be angry about. By applying our responses towards a peaceful resolution we can use our natural abilities to find the fulfilment we crave. We may well have worked hard on ourselves prior to this stage and we can at last gain a sense of success and victory with the energy that this card brings. Rather than weakness and failure we find balance and strength. This can open up a sense of direction and hope for the future as this energy works through us and our lives.

SEVENS

This forward momentum from the six energy as it plays out takes us naturally then to the Seven. Here we have the number and energy that connects us to our fate and destiny, and can test and challenge us to help steer us toward our life-path and highest possible fulfilment. As such Seven can be seen as the number of our 'cosmic structure'.

Not least here is that human life is often broken up into seven periods of ten years each, giving us the Biblical score of thee score years plus ten as our allotted life span as well as Shakespeare's seven ages of man. The theme of seven continues across many of our lives, there being of course seven days to our week, the seventh being set apart for rest and even in today's mad, mad world it is still possible to sense something of this sacredness.

Many people experience the seven year itch and may take to one of the seven seas to escape their fate! They may even drink some 7-Up in celebration or break into song using all seven of the musical notes in the scale. They may journey to one of the seven major stars or feel they are following the seven paths of the Cross that Christ undertook. Further study would reveal a change in the Moon's phase every seven days.

Then it might be time to follow in Sinbad's footsteps and take one of his seven fabled journeys or see the Seven Wonders of the World whilst no doubt studying the seven colours of the rainbow. They might then read the tale of Snow White and her seven dwarves and partake in the seven liberal arts of mediaeval life that lifted us above the mundane.

From their studies they would soon see the many links between seven and magic, religion and superstition throughout history. Of course if they waited seven years they would find historically any debts would be wiped out, slaves would be freed and fields left fallow. Mathematically we can see seven as the blend of the spiritual three and the material four and know that seven is the only prime number that is not divisible.

The Baylonians built their pyramids with seven stories to reflect their seven main planets. The Mayans spoke of a seven layered sky and the Egyptians seven paths to heaven. This is perhaps the seven chakra system widely known today and may be why the Chinese linked the number seven to human and especially female, life.

Biblically seven also features strongly. The Old Testament tells us that Lamech came along seven years after Adam and lived for 777 years. Transgressions were avenged sevenfold. Solomon's Temple had seven steps to take you in and there being seven pillars of wisdom, while Noah's dove was away on its maiden flight for seven days. The Euphrates river was divided into seven brooks reflecting perhaps seven deadly sins or maybe gifts of the Holy Spirit and seven sacraments. Perhaps this is why there were seven lions in the den of Samson and why he had seven locks of his hair cut in the famous incident. Joshua had Jericho circles seven times with seven trumpeters to destroy it,

Marriage ceremonies gained seven blessings with both feasts and mournings lasting seven days showing us something of the power and energy of this number. Interestingly for our purposes here, mathematicians say that the highest possibility of randomness comes when cards are shuffled precisely seven times

So when we experience this energy in our cards and lives we often need to learn to trust what is within and trust the process of life. There can be a need to orientate our life around the workings of Spirit and act as a guide for others. The seven energy can make us seem aloof and distant as we do so, finding some aspects of the world hard to take. Our minds can become sharpened however as we respond to the deep, inner search we take now. So seven can become the number of the independent loner in need of their boundaries.

In the Pentacles Seven we can find we are challenged by the ways of the world, ultimately to find our place within it and to be who we are and do what is right for us to be doing. This can be a very worldly experience when we may need to muddy our hands in the quagmire of everyday tit and tattle. It can be a wearisome experience and it is good as a way to assess ourselves to check our level of energy now, to see if what we are doing has a tiring effect on us and if we are becoming depleted or whether what we do energises and inspires us, galvanising our forces to spur and motivate us onward, as of course, should be the case.

Challenges presented to us as we experience the energy of this card are of course opportunities to steer us in this right direction and allow us to work towards the fulfilment of our physical and everyday capability. So it may seem as if a great energy is required at least to begin with but this multiplies by itself the more we put in and in this we can learn a great lesson from the Universe.

We can also find with this energy that we may need to look back a little before we plunge forward. By looking at our past achievements we can seen the fruit of our efforts and make a clear assessment based on this as to where we wish to go next. Setting goals is important now as may well find we are shifting gears a little and our priorities changing, perhaps away from purely material achievement to something with a little more depth and our purpose for us as an individual. In this way we can achieve perhaps the most powerful product of this energy, being the ability to control our everyday life and shape our on destiny.

With the emotional energy of the Cups Seven applied, we can find that we need to determine truth from illusion. Just as with the Earth energy of the previous card here we are offered a chance to master ourselves emotionally. This can be a great challenge to many people but if we can learn to detach from our emotions even a little we immediately lesson the power and dominion they might appear to have over us. This can be done through meditation and breath work, as well as practices such as Chi Kung, Tai Chi and other forms of exercise.

The saying that 'still waters run deep' is brought to mind as we undergo the flow of this energy through us. We may indeed need to dig deep within our emotional resources and seek what is truth and known to us as fact and what is watered down and distorted by our feelings and pre-conceptions arising from them. Often painful and difficult in nature, we can however find that we can move beyond these things by looking at our motivation.

There are two basic impulses and emotional motivations in the human psyche, if we strip away all others and see these two as opposite ends of the same spectrum. These are fear and love. As I have quoted elsewhere, we can turn to the great and green Master Yoda when he says that 'fear leads to anger, anger leads to hate and hate leads to the dark side' that being here the distortion and illusion of emotional depth and depression. If however we can learn, as did Luke Skywalker when he encountered his nemesis full on in the cave (in this case in the form of his father, or at least his energy), that there 'is nothing to fear but fear itself', we can shift from a motivation of fear to one of love.

Then we can become soft and open, able to allow truth to come to us without falling to a deep depression or the depth of despair, or reaching for the bottle or whatever. In this we find a deeper strength and greater sense of power and control. We find then we can make choices and perhaps by acknowledging daily that we have a body, emotions and mind but our truth and being is energy, consciousness and will and that we are eternal, infinite and immortal we can continue to expand into emotional depth without fear but a soft heart full of compassion and love. (Acknowledgment to Stuart Wilde for the source of that).

As we assimilate this energy and knowledge we will find that the Universe supplies us more of what we draw to us, which in this case is emotional openness, honesty and indeed, love. Our rose-coloured glasses lose their shaded tint and reality opens up to us and we may find to our amazement that the world can be quite a beautiful place and so can many of those in it.

Inspiration and hope can be restored to the weary heart now, and release of past pain and fear can be allowed to slip away. We can literally, take heart now, and find kindness in cruelty and love within fear, sensing and feeling hope rather than despair.

The same can be said with the Swords Seven in its potential, working instead through our minds and offering us a different choice and way of thinking. Rather than seeing the bad in people and having an expectation of loss, betrayal and lies, we can choose instead to appeal to the best in others in order to get the best out of them, which is self-perpetuating energy that only grows and benefits all in its path.

We need to look at the darkness within our own mind to achieve this of course, for nothing sadly is that easy! However by acknowledging our mental fears and inadequacies and the incorrect and plainly bad decisions we have made in the past, we can let any guilt of them go, along with regret and its resultant sadness and instead allow ourselves to be free enough to make some different choices.

We may find as we absorb this energy that we seem to draw some people to us who are charlatans, liars and peddlers of seemingly too god to be true schemes and promises. Of course if something seems too good to be true it is usually because it is and so we learn the power of discernment and with this card specifically, truthful mental judgement.

Rather than using coercion and our powers of persuasion we can choose instead to detach and walk away from what we know and can see is not real, not honourable or exploitative. The detraction of our energy from this equation ensures that we are not drawn into the fallacy of lies and falsehood, which simply cannot ever succeed since the Universe is not based on that. It also has the effect of offering those who are trying this way to learn as we present them with the truth, both by our own actions and our words. We present our truth for ourselves quietly, calmly and clearly and we move on, leaving only our footprint behind.

With the Rods Seven the energy can be a little more direct as it moves through us, igniting our fire. We need to become tempered by this heat now, a little more rarefied and true to who and what we are.

As with the previous Sevens we can be presented with a choice here, and as we look at the traditional image of this card we can see that this can be defence or attack. Of course as we may already realise from what we have just recently learnt to defend is to fear and to attack, love. Of course attack does not mean here aggression in any way, but a determination, a force within ourselves that says we shall not be overcome, we have what it takes to win the battle within us and move forwards and onwards in our lives with hope in our hearts and positive expectation in our minds, making us a being of positively charged light and energy at this level. We can learn now that what we project is what we create and experience.

There is no time like the present, indeed now is all there is and as such the energy of this card galvanises us to act and act now. The expression of this fiery seven energy seems to motivate us forwards with a continuing and resolute force, power and belief that cannot help but result in success, of whatever it is we are focussed on. Of course we should check our conscience to ensure that where we are motivated is in keeping with the positive and loving workings of the Universe and then just go for it!

So here we learn to become in charge and in control of our own fate and destiny, to be secure and fully with our presence in our own body and in this world we have created. Next comes the recognition of what that fate might be, which Eight gives us, rather usefully.

EIGHTS

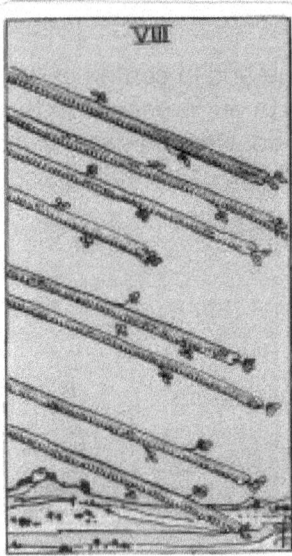 

Eight is regarded as a lucky number, since it is seen as existing beyond the seven spheres and fixed stars of our Universe. In this sense it is the level beyond the human experience, seen as over and above the energies of the seven chakras, hence its link with the fortunate. This may also be why the Babylonians saw eight as the number of the gods.

Similarly Mythras tells us that eight is the realm of the 'mountains of transubstantiation', being the eighth gate beyond the seventh. The Muslims also linked eight to Paradise, with seven hells but eight paradises. In India, Muslim gardens can be divided into eight areas to reflect this paradise. Islam has eight angels to carry the divine throne representing another link to the heavenly.

In the Sufi traditions there are eight basic rules expressed in eight sentences of the Path of Junayd. In China Confucianism gives us eight precious items in life and the Chinese divided life into stages based on the energies of eight – at eight months milk teeth appear and then are lost at eight years. We reach puberty in twice times eight years and lose our sexual virility at eight times eight years – apparently!

Buddhism teaches the eightfold path to enlightenment as a means to achieve cosmic equilibrium. In the Jewish tradition the eight day is that of purification and biblically, Christ gave us eight beatitudes in his Sermon on the Mount and was then resurrected on the eighth day of his Passion.

The figure eight is also similar of course to the basic shape and construction of the DNA molecule. We see this on the Magician card, in its horizontal form, known as the lemniscate, being a symbol for infinity and continuing, infinite life.

So just as four is the number of the manifest and created world this is doubled to give us the eight, for greater power. When working with the eight energy then we need to learn how to handle and use that power and apply the achievement and success in the service of the common good. Eight energy tends to bring us issues of dealing with worldly power and to reconcile our inner drives to succeed with any fear of actually doing this. There is a need for inner abundance, power and respect for our ability as we learn to establish rules we can follow to achieve the success we long for. In this way we rise above the crowd and so can present a spiritual fulfilment manifested in a concrete form in the everyday, material world. So with seven we see our fate and at eight we absorb and act upon it, and start to live and fulfil it.

This is perhaps no more clearly shown than with the Pentacles Eight, the traditional card of the hard-working craftsman. The energy here is certainly one of worldly achievement and we can see that the need here is to remain grounded and in control of what one is doing. Effort and concentration are required as we seek to act our intended fate and destiny now that we have discovered this. It can be common to feel a certain quickening of one's energy here, an acceleration of our force and power as we align ourselves to what we are here to do and naturally ignite our passion as well as our natural ability. All these become streamlined and we can start to experience the knowledge and reality that we really can achieve anything we want to.

We can apply our expertise now and we can also find that others may come to us to learn and to seek our knowledge, In these days of heightened energies and planetary alignments we can certainly find that there will always be those lacking in their energy who might like to steal a little of our own where it's freely available. With the energy of this card this can occur if we allow it, giving us a further challenge to rise to remain in keeping our focus and a hold of our power so that this vampiristic tendency does not come to suck us dry!

The more honest we are the more in keeping with natural flow we will find ourselves now. There can be a need for a 'giveaway' too, to not only avoid greed but also to maximise that natural and Universal flow. By allowing ourselves to donate to charitable or community causes we open ourselves to a greater flow of energy and since we are here in the realm of money and work, it is good we do something for nothing and give away some of what we have. This allows us to learn the truth that we are much stronger and greater when combined and working as a collective than individually.

Emotionally we experience this energy as something of an inner call to assert our individuality and independence. It is perhaps for this reason that traditional images show someone walking away from what they have been attached to at an emotional level. However when we look deeper and more therapeutically we can see that what is being experienced is actually emotional stability. As we strive to establish our own feelings and learn to accept them, whatever they may be so we find we do not rely on others in order to feel good.

Instead we find an inner strength that allows for us to be who we are, and perhaps most importantly, love ourselves just as we are. Of course the more we can do this, the more secure and strong we feel in being able to express that love for each other and celebrate the connectedness that exists between us. This is the energy flow of the Cups Eight.

So we can find deeper and stronger emotions moving through us now and we can have a need to step away from them a little and learn to be objective so we are not just swept along with the next tide of emotion that flows our way. This does not mean we deny or ignore our emotions of course, and in fact it is rather the opposite. By knowing we have the independence and strength to embrace those feelings, we find we can transmute and move beyond them. We can simply look at what we are feeling, knowing it does not threaten to destroy us, accept it for what it is and choose how we respond.

This is at once empowering and creates a deepening of the emotional energy flow through us, Because of this independence and objectivity we may find that we can or need to walk away and cut ties with some aspects of our behaviour as well as from certain situations and people in our life. There is a sense of emotionally moving on as we allow the energy of this card to do its thing. The deeper energies we connect to are like a well within us, reaching to unknown and bottomless depths; a source of emotional power beyond understanding.

The same can be true mentally of course with the Sword Eight. Here we can learn the art of correct thinking and just as with our hearts previously, we can find something of the power of the mind, not just from practising the art of positive thinking, as we might expect, useful and productive though this is. Rather though as we move away from fear and into the softness and openness that is love, so we can see that there is nothing to fear from our minds, and that our thoughts are only that and of themselves cannot destroy us.

Again, as we learn some dominion over our thought processes so we can learn that same independence with our mind as with our heart that allows us to let our thoughts come and go, holding on to no resistance and indeed not holding on to our thoughts at all. As we open our minds to this freedom so we can fully embrace the power of our own individual mind and perhaps for the first time, truly learn to think for ourselves and consequently make our own decisions. As we put this into practice so it is we become ever more the architect of our own lives and the mast of our own destiny in this lifetime, just as we are called and challenged to do.

We can really see a choice that we can make with both Cups and Swords Eight, that of victim or creator. If we allow them to, our feelings and our thoughts can imprison us. If we can muster just a little courage from within though we can find a freedom from the prison as the energy here does it work through us and we think and feel freely and abundantly.

So it is we come to the fiery level of this energy with the Rods Eight. Here we can learn to temper those impulses and irrational tendencies and absorb with the energy of this card a greater sense within us that we can call cognisance; the art of just knowing. To begin with we can be creatures of instinct and impulse, swayed and knocked in various different directions by each that comes our way. When however we experience this card's flow and lesson, we can learn to sit with those tendencies as they come to us and begin to sense deep within the core of our being that we just know the right thing to do. We cannot necessarily explain this but as we slip into our own natural flow this is one of the natural results.

We can find then that we fall into doing things spontaneously and without delay since we just sense the right timing and act; no other considerations are necessary. This is the result of when we learnt to accelerate our own energies, not getting side-tracked or bogged down by our emotions or our thoughts but operating at an accelerated level whilst remaining grounded, which produces within us that sense of knowing. Once aligned with this, all that is required is some effort and commitment to do whatever is necessary in our selves and lives to maintain that focus and maintain our energies at as high and clear a level as we can achieve for this to continue. It then operates through us without resistance and we experience the full energy of Rods Eight, living and being just as we are intended to.

NINES

Once we do this then we can shift headlong into the Nine energies. This is seen as the sacred three energy magnified, along with the energy of Eight added to, so the beatitude there is lifted and expanded to, giving Nine its resultant euphoric energy of fulfilment and achievement. Here we are as far as we can go with the single digit numbers so in essence this is the end of the road, the peak of the hill and highest point we can achieve and from where we can see and survey all that lies before us and from whence we have come.

The energy of Nine also has a connection with suffering however, perhaps from Christ who died at 3pm, being nine hours after sunrise or the god Odin who hung on the World Tree for nine days and nights to learn nine songs and to rule over nine worlds.

More common however are associations with nine that speak of that achievement and a link to higher and cosmic worlds and a higher level of life. There are said to be nine orders of angels as well as nine branches of the cosmic tree. The Persian and Turkish traditions speak of nine skies whilst the Muslims have nine states of existence. In China nine is connected with heaven and nine kinds of harmony with the sage Lao Tzu said to be born 9 x 9 years after he was conceived.

The Mongol community required people to prostrate themselves before the Great Khan nine times, who was attended by nine standards. To the Turks there were nine spheres of existence and 'nothing beyond nine'. In their society rather enticingly presents were given in group of nine. The Celts took nine steps to measure distance and only when this far away from a dwelling would a fire be lit. Both the Celts and Germans followed a nine day period in their legal systems.

Many initiatory rites followed a nine energy too. The Elusinian mysteries required a nine day initiation and it apparently took nine days to travel through the Greek underworld. The Egyptians honoured nine gods as well as nine manifest principles with the Pharoah being represented by nine archers' bows. Interestingly the Freemason founders of the US Government used the Egyptian Ennead or nine fold rule in their laws.

Biblically we are told that God spoke to Abraham when he was 99 and the Hebrew meaning of 'Amen' being 'so be it' having a numerical value of 99 when calculated. Elsewhere Demeter searched through the underworld for 9 months and Persephone was sentenced to spend nine months of each year above ground. The goddess Brighid was attended by nine maidens and the Beltane fires of the Celts attended by nine groups of nine men.

Nine features in folk tales to, most notably the Pied Piper of Hamlyn who lured the children away with the ninth tune of his flute. Of course we know too that a stitch in time saves nine, which takes us to cloud nine so long as we are dressed to the nines and prepared to go the whole nine yards, possession of course being nine tenths of the law.

Since nine operates at this high energetic level it follows that when we work with its energy in ourselves and lives we must do so in accord with our highest integrity and ethics. With this energy we are challenged to align our lives with our natural intuitive wisdom and so inspire others. In short we can learn to live by example and like Ghandi said, be the change we wish to see. We need now to practice what we preach and to quote Ghandi again, demonstrate his maxim that 'my life is my teaching'. Nine energy allows us the chance to unite our mind and heart to access our innate higher wisdom. This leads us to the application of spiritual law.

With the Pentacles Nine we find this applied in a material sense of course, the energy here applying itself to the physical level of our being and life. Given that Nine brings us the highest energetic force numerically, it is easy to assume that this will materialise riches and abundance in our lives. Indeed the fortune-tellers will often predict this but what we must also realise is that this can and will only come about, (should indeed that even be our target), when we find that same state of richness within.

Primarily this comes about from learning to love and value ourselves and what we do with our everyday, practical lives and bodies. How much do you think you're worth? When you begin to feel priceless or beyond monetary value, you're getting it. It's not enough to just tell yourself this however or even just feel it within; you must know it with each and every fibre of your being. No matter what you may do for work or not as the case may be, the energy of this card comes from a life that shows abundance in all things.

We must be careful of avarice and greed with this energy too since we frail humans have a tendency to get carried away with ourselves and go over the top. We usually find then that any physical gain, pleasure and comfort is temporary and great loss follows great gain. Better to achieve a more lasting state of achievement within and satisfaction with our lives. Self-gratification should be avoided and opportunities for sharing and service looked for instead.

A good means of measure when experiencing the energy of this card is to monitor our own energy levels. Since the number here is the highest then it follows we should also experience abundant energy levels and perhaps feel an acceleration of our bodies' abilities, reserves and capabilities. This all comes when we are 'in our power' and moving with the natural flow of energy we attract to ourselves.

If we do allow ourselves to fall open to greed or abuse of the richness that this energy brings then we can equally find a plummeting of our energy levels, as if we have exhausted the flow coming to us, Whilst this is not really the case what can happen is that we deplete our reserves and come at things from the wrong angle, ego takes over and we let the power we have corrupt us. We would certainly not be the first in this of course, but what matters is how quickly we can spot this and remedy it.

Given that we are at the physical level of life here a good analogy is that of the athlete, who puts in a tremendous amount of work to develop his body and his ability and fine tunes it to such a high level to win medals and so on. However it is precisely because of this fine tuning that it is so much more prone to injury as a result of going too far and pushing too much. Better then to relax and go with the natural flow, using what comes to us to help keep on top of things rather than ending up on the treatment table of life!

Emotionally these same dangers are present too but let us not dwell on potentials and pitfalls too much, for this card also brings with it the propensity for a fulfilment far beyond what we may have ever felt before and can leave us feeling, if not invincible then certainly on top of the world and this is always a good thing! The Cups Nine energy brings with it a chance to 'eat, drink and be merry' and enjoy the good things of life.

At the emotional level we can find that we are unusually full of beans, always with a ready smile to crack and a joke to make. We find we can see reasons to be happy in circumstances that may previously have brought us down. Positivity seems to flow through our pores and have the same uplifting effect on those we come into contact with. We find a generosity of spirit within ourselves as if our cups does indeed 'runneth over'.

Love can be experienced in its fullest measure now and it is how we choose to respond to this that can tell us much about our learning with this energy, or otherwise. The nature of love is not to possess and is not for the self so how we allow ourselves to express that which we feel within becomes important to the successful application and assimilation of this energy. If we are able to use this by way of service rather than self this energy can bring us much by way of real happiness and serenity within.

Of course the emptiness and hollow feelings that can result from the abuse of this energy can bring us so very low that we may feel we have no worth at all, let alone anything to offer anyone else. Here we need to take from this energy a certain resilience and strength from depth in our feeling to know that whatever else we may have, we always have ourselves and here we can learn to love ourselves no matter what. This can be a real strength in times of challenge, trouble and loss that this energy also brings.

The nature of Nine energy is then rather like the proverbial double-edged sword. Of course the Sword Nine emphasises this, giving us a choice ultimately, of how to see things, positively or negatively. There can be such an abundance of thought flowing through us when we experience this cards energy that it can literally drive us crazy if we do not respond well.

Inspiration may flow through us at a rate of knots and monitored closely for quality control, can produce some wonderful creations, of whatever kind. We may have such a flow of thought that sleep becomes a hard thing to come by as we seek to turn our minds off. Even when we do achieve that rare and blissful state we can then find we have much more conscious recall of many weird and wonderful dreams than is usual, as the deeper levels of our mind seek to sift and sort the wheat from the chaff of our everyday, conscious thought processes.

Here the need is to temper that flow with a pause, to breathe and become still and open ourselves gently to a more manageable flow of mental energy. Meditation can certainly help here, along with breathing techniques of whatever kind we may choose.

It is as if someone has lifted the veil from our thoughts now and we may feed ourselves books aplenty, drinking the words and concept down like a good wine. Understanding comes to us but we have our limits and must seek peace, calm and quiet to allow all that we learn and open ourselves to now, to sink in and become part of that knowledge that we possess from here on.

Discipline of thought is required or we may lose our way to falsehood and illusion. The result of this is worry and mental insecurity and even instability if we continue to allow things to go unchecked. We may despair at times but the energy here also shows us the silver lining if we but choose to see it. We are challenged now to develop a positive mental attitude in all things and to know, accept and understand the truth of things for us.

As we learn this we open ourselves to the great strength that can come with the Rods Nine. Again, it can seek to destroy us if we cannot handle or cope with it but there is a great opportunity here too to arrive at a higher spiritual level than we have previously reached.

Since Rods is the suit in the Tarot that connects us to our will, to our inner drive and determination then it follows that with the strongest energy here, we can find ourselves quite literally, fired up. Again, it is a matter of how we respond to that energy that tells us a great deal and whether we have responded to the challenge here and 'got the message'.

The card often depicts a weary worker at the end of his day. However there would have been a time earlier on in the day when he felt the warmth of the sun flowing into his bones, fuelling his efforts and energies and sustaining him as we worked. It is this state, again of flow and fortune if you will, that is the indication of successful assimilation of the energy here.

This energy is the culmination of the journey through numerical Minor Arcana cards and so it is here that we experience the full flow and force of our expression. Fuelled by this we can find that as we adapt ourselves to what comes to us we can remain open and relaxed in our lives, soft of heart and mind resulting in this accelerated flow of energy through all levels of our being, giving us the height of both achievement and satisfaction.

With this energy we can align ourselves to our own Tao if you will, our own Way, whatever this might be for us, it being an individual thing. There is a natural inspiration and out flow from our following our Way but we cannot preach or teach others, only by example can we demonstrate our Way and this can naturally flow to others and reveal theirs to them.

We need the courage that can come with the energy of this card as we draw in more and more of our natural flow and inner strength. Directed correctly we can find that conflict drops away from us, within and without in our lives and our enthusiasm for life can know no bounds. Completely open and at a level of oneness with ourselves and life we absorb what we need, respond to this and find fulfilment.

TENS

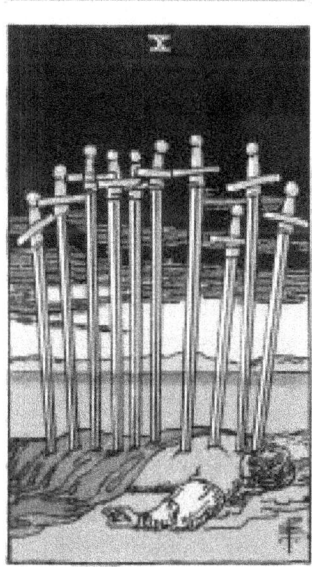

This takes us naturally to the energy of Ten. With this we reach the end of each suit of course but we need not think here in terms of endings, rather new beginnings and a shift to a different level. This may be a move to another level of our being as we embark on a different suit or an encounter with a Major Arcana energy. What we experience is a mastery or control of the energy of the suit to which the card belongs. Ten is One plus Zero, so the individual is led back to unity, but at a higher level. Pythagoras told us that Ten beings fulfilment and brings all other numbers and energies to perfection.

So the energy of Ten is seen as limitless. This is seen from it being beyond the horizon that Nine represents but added to, so becomes unlimited. Ten can also be seen as the energy of the parental One and Two with their seven children and so is a portrait of all the numbers together, or a synergy of everything. From the ancient Numerologists point of view Ten contains everything we need to come to know the construction and workings of the Universe.

Across the world the Buddhists saw Ten as the number of perfections that exist and the Egyptians saw Ten qualities in all created forms. The Sufi told us there were Ten veils that separated us from seeing our divinity whilst the Hebrew Qaballah has Ten Sephiroth or spheres which were stages of unfoldment on the path to enlightenment. Biblically there are Ten Commandments whilst Noah came ten generations after Adam and ten generations later we have Abraham. Egypt was also assailed by ten plagues before the Exodus and there are said to be ten spiritual graces.

Ten is also around us in nature, starting with our ten fingers and toes and our decimal system. Lobsters and crayfish have ten walking legs and a squid has ten tentacles. The passion flower has ten petals and many citrus fruits have ten segments to their whole.

Experience of the 'perfect ten' is akin to making something ten times better, whilst to be decimated means something is reduced by a tenth of its standing or power. A round number brings it to the nearest multiple of ten and we can tithe by giving a tenth of our income. Major celebrations occur on each tenth birthday, especially so when we reach the 'big 40'!

When working with the ten energy we are called to embrace, accept and use our inner gifts and it is for each to find their own and learn to assimilate and express whatever it may be. Let's see how we do this with each card.

With Pentacles Ten we can absorb the energy offered to us and find that we can reach a stage of practical fulfilment hitherto unknown. This means that we can come to know our true passion and spend our time following it. Of course in these days we all need to pay bills and earn money but this energy if we use it wisely can allow us do that as well as following our passion, whatever that might be.

The energy here can bring stability and comfort as well as offering us success in our endeavours. This may not be measured in only worldly terms of course but in terms of satisfaction and a sense of achievement, giving us a serenity within with how we are spending our time. We can feel contented now with the part we are playing in the world.

There may be a great deal for us to do now, for this is an energy that is strong and can make us very busy, but we will not be lacking in motivation, energy or ability to carry out the tasks before us. Indeed this energy can give us a degree of power that can also serve as a challenge and opportunity to learn. Power as we know, corrupts and as we embrace our own individual practical and worldly power so it is we must come to learn to avoid greed or abuse any of the privileges we may have earned or come by now. Humility and grace are the keys to this, both traits that can seem sadly lacking in today's egotistical society.

Service can and should become a priority as we assimilate the Pentacles Ten energy. The more we give the more we will find we can receive. Remember that the energy of Ten takes us beyond the horizon of the Nine and so it is we should move beyond aggrandisement and worldly highs now. Our achievement and security need to come from higher ideals and goals and this can often primarily take the form of guiding, teaching, healing and helping others.

The energy of Cups Ten can bring feelings we often will not have experienced before. The term serenity is possibly best applied here. This is not because we have finally got all that we wanted or even that we have found the right person with whom we wish to spend the rest of our lives. Rather it is because that no matter what our circumstances or situation, no matter what external chaos we may face , within ourselves we have reached a level of acceptance, understanding and above all love, that gives us an unshakeable calm.

This is not easily achieved of course and we may find we only get glimpses of it on our journey through life. However once afforded even the briefest glimpse of it, we know that this state can exist within us and as we experience the energy of this card so it is we can come to know this more fully and more consciously than ever before.

Much of the key to absorbing this energy so it stays with us all the time in a tangible way is learning to love and forgive ourselves, no matter what. This is not an excuse to behave as we wish and then feel bad about it! Rather we can take the energy here and use it to set ourselves the highest standard of moral and ethical behaviour and do our utmost to stick by it. As we learn to love ourselves for who and what we are so grace is given and if we can accept this and remain soft and open within our hearts so we can learn the message of this card.

We can find emotional stability now and often this can manifest in our relationships, family and friendships. The fullness of emotion can be seen as satisfaction and we must guard against a sense of laziness or idleness here, lest we think we have got as far as we can go and need do nothing more. Then we have missed the message that it is only by continued effort and continually listening to our conscience that we can hope to retain that serenity and satisfaction in our heart that is the hallmark of the energy of this card.

Traditionally Swords Ten shows us a distressing scene of a figure lying prone and bleeding on the ground having been stabbed in the back. The implication here is of ruin and defeat, but therapeutically we can see a different message when we turn to the underlying energy of the card.

We know already that the energy of Ten is concerned with fulfilment, understanding and subsequent release. Here this applies itself to the mind of course, through the Element of Air. So it is we can see that the energy of this card can offer us instead a release

118

from mental anguish and suffering, through understanding and acceptance. This can bring about the peace of mind possible to achieve through this energy as we learn to let go mentally and know that we cannot always have all the answers and find an acceptance of this.

So many find that they go through periods of mental anguish, torment and suffering but it is through these times that we often find the answers and better responses to our dilemmas, whatever they may be for each of us. Swords Ten can bring both of these, for it represents the full package mentally. We find now that we can receive a new sharpness and clarity of mind that serves us in good stead as we face our mental demons and monsters and turn them into something more friendly.

The energy here is really one of realisation, as the new light of understanding dawns within our minds and regardless of our problems or the mysteries that may seem to surround us, we have understanding and knowledge within that tells us our situation will change for this is the very nature of life. So it is we can have peace at all times within as we absorb the energy here, which is surely a very great gift,

Acceptance of truth can be a key here, as a veil may be lifted from our minds as we absorb the energy now. The clarity that can result can cause us to need to make some admission to ourselves but as we open ourselves to this rather than fighting it we can find that peace of mind that is beyond all understanding and take us to a new place, of calm acceptance and mental serenity.

Last of all on our journey through the landscape of the Minor Arcana numbered cards we come to the Rods Ten. Again the traditional image shows an unfortunate victim of an overdose of the world and its ways. Exhaustion and oppression seem to be the themes we can see but when we look at an appropriate use of the energy from this card we can instead find that we can rise above that which would seek to keep us from being all that we might be.

Ten can more easily and appropriately be seen as an energy of triumph and success. Here at the Rods level of our inner fire we find that we can tap into a source of inspiration, drive, ambition and will that can cause us to feel we are invincible and unstoppable. There is an excellent affirmation that occurs here, that sums up the inner state achievable from the energy of this card, to which I must acknowledge the author and tutor Stuart Wilde as the source of. This is:

I have a body but I am more than my body
I have emotions but I am more than my emotions
I have a mind but I am more than my mind
I am a being of energy, consciousness and will
I am eternal, infinite and immortal.

Once this truth is fully absorbed and realised we can then say we have done the same with the energy, message and lesson of this card. Motivation can be a hard thing to come by at times, often preceded by our not even knowing what we should motivate ourselves for! By the time we have reached the stage of this card on our journey however, we should be fully conscious and aware of where our passion and talents in this life lie. Now with the advent of the flow of this energy stream towards us we find that we can tap into an enormous well of power and motivation that will never leave.

Of course and as the image of this card can show we need to guard against going over the top with this and exhausting ourselves. It should be made clear here that the energy we can tap into is limitless and we cannot deplete or exhaust this, only ourselves. However with the correct discipline and approach we can induce within ourselves a flow of energy that keeps us going. We can find we need less sleep for we are working to an optimum flow of energy now that lifts us above the mundane, accelerates our living and raises our energy. Health is abundant, so are achievements and we live a life of fulfilment, whatever we turn our individual talents and abilities to.

Inner strength and the stamina to go with it are natural sources within us now and so it is we seem to glide effortlessly through our lives. Not in a sense of the avoidance of hard work and effort but with a sense of measured application and flow, as if we are simply following the natural order of things, with no doubt, fear or worry to slow us down or dilute the manner in which we conduct ourselves.

So it is we reach the destination on our map, the arrival home from our long and at points seemingly unending quest. Indeed it is as if we stepped out from our safe and familiar homes many moons go and have travelled far and wide across a landscape, of our own individual making, that has in turns delighted, appalled, shocked and challenged us in ways that we may never have agreed to undertake the journey at all had we known what lay ahead.

It is rather like I tell the students who are alternatively brave or foolish enough to study my Tarot Therapy courses – life teaches you about the Tarot and Tarot teaches you about life. I tell them that they really get two courses in one – study of the Tarot and study of themselves. Lastly I also warn them that by the end of the course they will be different to how they are at the start. Just as here as we return to our homes, weary but wiser, we find it is familiar and yet somehow different. It is only when we realise that the home has not changed, but we have, that we get the point.

CHAPTER 5 – HOME FROM THE QUEST

So here we are some three volumes and many years later that we finally arrive back home at the completion of our quest. Weary but wiser we can finally plonk ourselves down before the fire, put our feet up and take a well-deserved rest.

It is my hope that you have seen at least something of what the Tarot can be when applied just a little differently than future prediction. Since the time I began working on Volume 1 of Tarot Therapy we have seen the rise and rise of telephone psychic lines and the media backing that accompanies them. This has again changed the image of the Tarot, what it is and how it is used.

Sadly it seems that the Tarot has become accepted in this role and indeed it must be said, by many of its practitioners too. It is now possible to forge oneself a career from the comfort of your armchair, something about which I intend to write next! Whilst it is true that these telephone services have spread awareness of the Tarot, it is my view that this has also resulted in a lower common denominator in the regard people have for it as well as what it can do when used in a more professional and therapeutic environment. This is not to say that all such services are unprofessional but when the client cannot even see the cards then we must immediately and inevitably lose something of the therapeutic power and energy of the cards. It should be said here too that I am sure that many of the readers would prefer to see their clients personally but it is simply a case of 'needs must' for them. Equally though, just because something can be done, does not mean it should.

My point here however is not to decry telephone psychic lines but rather to bemoan the current state and image of the Tarot in general but hopefully conclude with an optimism for what lies ahead for these noble cards. From my standpoint the Tarot seems in many ways to be in a rather sorry state. This is not the cards themselves; I have far too much love and respect for them to think that. But it is the regard they are held in by the masses that I feel needs to change and the manner in which they are portrayed in the media including and perhaps especially that supposedly sympathetic to spiritual matters. When this begins we can begin to shift the consciousness of what the Tarot is and what it does.

Currently though, every time I see a new book on the Tarot released it seems to follow the same now tired formula, with some introductory comments, usually covering that authors interpretation of the origins of the Tarot, followed by one page and one page only on each card, showing its symbolism and what it means in a reading, including of course which way up it faces. Next we get a few spreads, these days normally accompanied by a case study for each one, to demonstrate how brilliant the spread is!

It is certainly acknowledged that each of these tomes has something to offer and we can always learn but again I despair at times that we can find no new way of demonstrating our love for and knowledge of the Tarot and the consequent effect of our efforts on the public that read our works. There are exceptions to this rather caustic view of Tarot publishing and these are applauded and warmly welcomed.

I must also mention the quite amazing number of Tarot decks that are appearing these days too – to which I intend to add my own efforts before too long! Again, many of these tend to reflect only a current trend or interest in an area, popularised by film and television, such as the many Gothic and Vampire based decks now available. Not to single these dark offerings out in any way but what I find is that the quality does not match quantity and this seems a great shame. It will have usually taken the creator many years of work to produce their work but they can often appear as a mere mass-produced factory product, with cheap looking artwork and a tawdry book of interpretations to accompany them.

To my eyes these all seem a variation on a theme and some of those themes seem to cling somewhat precariously and inappropriately to the title of Tarot. I am not including here the ever expanding number of 'Oracles' that are popping up now, as I cannot regard these as Tarot decks, even if, in some cases they use the title, presumably as a means of notching up a few more sales.

Indeed it seems that it is the forces of commercialism that are running riot and rough shod over the beautiful map of our sacred cards. Just like the rainforest and green spaces of our natural world, where there is money to be made, all else seems to come second.

So where in this can we find a hope for the reclamation of our sacred land and our sacred cards? I find that as I search ever more widely and deeply on that Jedi-like force called the internet that there are a growing number of folk who have an excellent professional and sacred understanding of the cards and what they are. Some of these are clever and dedicated enough to produce their own decks, with a care and conduct that undermines that of the bigger and established publishing houses.

Here for me lies hope. It is in the independence and freedom that the internet offers that we may find a way forward where those that 'get it' can show the rest of us why and how. As these brave folk move ever forward on their own quest so it may be that others who follow will journey further and deeper into the landscape and find new treasures within. Perhaps this will be a way that those of us who are not driven and motivated only by profit, but have a higher ideal at heart, can educate others as to the real and sacred nature of the Tarot and explore ways in which it can be used for the good and of course so much than seeing whether the boyfriend is coming back or some such.

My own journey with the Tarot will I think never end in this lifetime (at least). For some and still unknown reason I became fascinated with the cards as a teenager and now, thirty years later I am probably more fascinated - or should that be obsessed? It seems for me that when it comes to the Tarot the more I know, the more I want to know. Fortunately when it comes to the Tarot it seems that you can never stop learning.

There are many Tarot related projects on my 'to do' list and it is my hope that I remain healthy and whole enough to see at least some of them see the light of day. I am sure that others will add to the rich pantheon of Tarot related offerings and together we will create a marvellous and bejewelled Tapestry of Tarot. In the meantime I look forward to what is to come, hopefully without my dropping too many stitches along the way.

It should perhaps be mentioned here that what I have presented across what became the three volumes of Tarot Therapy is really only scratching the surface. I realised this when on nearing the completion of this last volume I felt dissatisfaction. When I examined this I found it was because I felt I had not said all I wanted to say about the cards and their energies, in terms of their interpretation.

Whilst this is good since it provides me with more fuel for more books it also made me realise that the full experience of the energy of each card cannot be put into words. Like the nature of energy itself, the Tarot simply is, and it is our individual experience of it in that moment that gives it interpretation. So I return to the idea that the Tarot cards do not mean anything.

In this they also mean everything, but only to the recipient or client at the time they are experiencing any one cards' energy in themselves and their life. To this person they will fully understand what the card means, but this does not mean it will mean the same for someone else or even themselves at a different time. In this way they cannot be explained, only experienced (though this won't stop me for one, trying!).

So more can, will and indeed should be said about the Tarot. Hopefully as we go the image and regard of the cards will rise and they can reclaim something of their sacred nature. It occurs to me that in this they reflect our regard for life itself and what is contained within it, for each of us. So it that the Tarot continues to serve each and every one of us if we were but to allow it. For me, there is no better service and no better teacher.

TAROT THERAPY PRODUCTS

Steve Hounsome produces a range of products and services, which are detailed below –

TAROT THERAPY TRAINING
There are three courses available, for those wishing to train as a Tarot Therapist –

- **INTRODUCTION** – For the complete beginner
- **CERTIFICATE** – For those wanting to read professionally for others
- **DIPLOMA** - For those wanting to develop their existing knowledge and ability

TAROT THERAPY READINGS
Steve is available for readings either in person in Dorset, England, by 'phone or by email.

PERSONAL, PSYCHIC & SPIRITUAL DEVELOPMENT
Steve has produced a range of meditations and exercises for personal, psychic and spiritual development. These are available as cd's or as downloads from the website.

MEDITATION, PSYCHIC DEVELOPMENT & TAROT STUDY GROUPS
Steve runs groups in all the above subjects, as well as holding a series of workshops throughout the year, in Dorset, England,

Full details of all the above are available at Steve's website –

www.tarottherapy.co.uk

You can also email Steve at –

steve@tarottherapy.co.uk

BIBLIOGRAPHY

Christina Bjergo – The Tao of Tarot, O Books, 2010
Tom Chetwynd – A Dictionary of Symbols, Paladin, 1982
J E Cirlot – A Dictionary of Symbols, Routledge, 1988
Dr Wayne W Dyer – Change Your Thoughts, Change Your Life, Hay House, 2007
Anna-Marie Ferguson – A Keeper of Words, Llewellyn 1995
Cynthia Giles – The Tarot Methods, Mastery and More, Simon & Schuster 1996
Steve Hounsome – Taming the Wolf: Full Moon Meditations, Capall Bann, 1995
Steve Hounsome – Practical Meditation, Capall Bann, 1996
Steve Hounsome – Practical Spirituality, Capall Bann, 1997
Steve Hounsome – Tarot Therapy Vol. 1, Capall Bann, 1999
Paul Huson – Mystical Origins of the Tarot, Destiny Books, 2004
Docters Van Leeuwen, Onno and Rob – The Complete New Tarot, Sterling Publishing Co. 1995
Dan Millman – The Life You Were Born to Live, H J Kramer 1993
John C Parkin – Fuck It, The Ultimate Spiritual Way, Hay House, 2007
Caroline Myss, Anatomy of the Spirit, Bantam Books 1997
Robert M Place – The Tarot History, Symbolism, and Divination, Penguin 2005
Anthony Robbins – Awaken The Giant Within, Pocket Books, 1991
AnneMarie Schimmel – The Mystery of Numbers, Oxford University Press, 1993
Michael S Schneider – A Beginners Guide to Constructing the Universe, Harper Collins, 1994
Steve Taylor – Waking From Sleep, Hay House, 2010

BIOGRAPHY

Steve Hounsome has been involved in this field for over thirty years and has completed a wide variety of studies and activities in this time.

Steve holds qualifications in the following subjects –

* *Progressive Healing*
* *Psychic Studies*
* *Esoteric Soul Healing*
* *Tarot*
* *Bach Flower Remedies*
* *Basic Counselling Skills*

The training Steve has completed is as follows –

* *One year Progressive Healing, Sanctuary of Progress*
* *One year Psychic Studies, Sanctuary of Progress*
* *Meditation - 2 years, private tutor*
* *Natural Magic, 1 year, Marian Green*
* *Ritual Magic, 1 year, The London Group*
* *Esoteric Soul Healing, 2 years, Isle of Avalon Foundation*
* *Bach Flower Remedies - Foundation Level Certificate*
* *Order of Bards, Ovates and Druids - 12 years, now initiated Druid member*

Steve has also attended lectures and workshops too numerous to mention over the years and continues to add to his knowledge and experience by attending events as they occur and maintaining his own regular sacred practices in Meditation, Yoga and Chi Kung.

Steve has had articles published in many magazines, on a variety of the subjects he works in. These include Positive Health and Pagan Dawn, as well as many of the smaller titles produced in the Pagan and holistic communities.

Steve has appeared on TV, twice alongside Derek Acorah on Granada TV's show 'Psychic Livetime' and acted as examiner on the Living TV series 'Jane Goldman Investigates', overseeing the work of Michelle Knight who taught the Tarot to Jane.

Steve acted as advisor and consultant for the New World 'Music of the Tarot' CD, for which he also wrote the accompanying booklet.

Steve has had eight books published –

* *Taming the Wolf: Full Moon Meditations*
* *Practical Meditation*
* *Practical Spirituality*
* *How To Be A Telephone Psychic*
* *Tarot Therapy Vol. 1: Tarot for the New Millenium*
* *Tarot Therapy Vol 2: Major Arcana, The Seekers Quest*
* *Tarot Therapy Vol. 3: Minor Arcana, The Map of the Quest*
* *The Tarot Therapy Deck*

Steve has also produced his own unique card sets –

* *The Tarot Therapy Cards*
* *Chakra Affirmation Cards*
* *Tarot Therapy Affirmation Cards*

Steve has also produced a range of 15 highly-acclaimed Meditation and Development CD's, which you can see full details of in the Shop on this website.

Steve is currently working on his own 'Tarot Therapy' deck and plans to produce a major new workbook, called 'Sacred Living'.

Steve has taught in person across the South of England and by distance learning internationally. Apart from his own private events, Steve has taught at Adult Education Centres in Hampshire and was tutor of the 2-year Tarot course at the prestigious 'Isle of Avalon Foundation' in Glastonbury, Somerset. Steve has tested and trained psychic readers for some of the leading telephone psychic companies in the UK, working across the world.

Steve was a Founder Member and Secretary of the Professional Tarot Society and was also Secretary of the British Psychic Registration Board, although both these organisations are no longer in existence. Steve is now a member of the following organisations –

* Order of Bards, Ovates and Druids (Steve acts as mentor for those following their training programme)
* *Spiritual Workers Association*
* *Tarot Association of the British Isles*
* *British Astrologers and Psychics Society*
* *Tarot Professionals*

Though a member of these Groups, Steve's approach to spirituality is an eclectic one, as he feels that every path has something to offer. He reads widely on spiritual subjects and incorporates what he learns into his teaching, in its various forms. Steve feels that a sense of the sacred for each individual is vital to the maintenance of health and well-being and for the fulfilment of our potential, development and life purpose. More personally, Steve has a deep love of many forms of music, runs long-distance and cycles. He enjoys visiting sacred and natural sites, plays tennis, attends his local gym regularly as well as watching football, remaining loyal to his origins by supporting his home-town team, Brighton & Hove Albion. He is the father of two children, Dakota and Amber.

www.ingramcontent.com/pod-product-compliance
Lightning Source LLC
Chambersburg PA
CBHW072146090426
42739CB00013B/3292